DATE DUE			
MAY 0 6 1995	JUN 1 0 2011		
MAY 1 3 1995			
AUG 1 8 1997			
OCT 1 7 1998			
FEB 0 2 1999			
APR 0 6 1999			
FEB 1 4 2000			
MAY 1 5 2000			
NOV 2 3 2010			
APR 1 3 2011			

Better Homes and Gardens®

Cookies for Kids

© Copyright 1983 by Meredith Corporation, Des Moines, Iowa.
All Rights Reserved. Printed in the United States of America.
First Edition. Seventh Printing, 1988.
Library of Congress Catalog Card Number: 82-80528
ISBN: 0-696-00867-X (hard cover)
ISBN: 0-696-00865-3 (trade paperback)

BETTER HOMES AND GARDENS® BOOKS

Editor: Gerald M. Knox
Art Director: Ernest Shelton
Managing Editor: David A. Kirchner

Food and Nutrition Editor: Doris Eby
Department Head—Cook Books: Sharyl Heiken
Senior Food Editor: Elizabeth Woolever
Senior Associate Food Editors: Sandra Granseth,
    Rosemary C. Hutchinson
Associate Food Editors: Jill Burmeister, Linda Foley,
    Linda Henry, Julia Malloy, Alethea Sparks, Marcia Stanley,
    Diane Yanney
Recipe Development Editor: Marion Viall
Test Kitchen Director: Sharon Stilwell
Test Kitchen Home Economists: Jean Brekke, Kay Cargill,
    Marilyn Cornelius, Maryellyn Krantz, Diana Nolin,
    Marge Steenson

Associate Art Director (Managing): Randall Yontz
Associate Art Directors (Creative): Linda Ford,
    Neoma Alt West
Copy and Production Editors: Nancy Nowiszewski,
    Lamont Olson, Mary Helen Schiltz, David A. Walsh
Assistant Art Directors: Harijs Priekulis, Tom Wegner
Graphic Designers: Mike Burns, Trish Church-Podlasek,
    Alisann Dixon, Mike Eagleton, Lynda Haupert, Deb Miner,
    Lyne Neymeyer, Stan Sams, D. Greg Thompson,
    Darla Whipple, Paul Zimmerman

Editor in Chief: Neil Kuehnl
Group Editorial Service Director: Duane L. Gregg
Executive Art Director: William J. Yates

General Manager: Fred Stines
Director of Publishing: Robert B. Nelson
Director of Retail Marketing: Jamie Martin
Director of Direct Marketing: Arthur Heydendael

COOKIES FOR KIDS

Editor: Jill Burmeister
Copy and Production Editor: David A. Walsh
Graphic Designer: Lyne Neymeyer
Illustrations: Thomas Rosborough

Our seal assures you that every recipe in *Cookies for Kids*
is endorsed by the Better Homes and Gardens Test
Kitchen. Each recipe is tested for family appeal, practicality,
and deliciousness.

On the cover: (clockwise from top) *Painted Easter Egg
Cookies* (see recipe, page 87), *Choose-a-Chip Oatmeal
Cookies* (see recipe, page 8), *Cut-It-Out Cookies* (see recipe,
page 44), and *Snapping Turtles* (see recipe, page 43).

Contents

Get Ready...Get Set...GO!

This book is especially for young cookie lovers. That means everything on these pages is fun—to read, to make, and to eat. Since adults are just grown-up kids, they'll like this book as much as youngsters will.

Kids, if you're making the cookies, be sure to have an adult help you. Using the help of a grown-up and the tips on these two pages, you'll turn out scrumptious cookies you'll be proud to say you made.

● **To measure liquids,** put a clear plastic or glass measuring cup on a level surface and bend down so your eyes are even with the measurement you need. Add liquid till it reaches the mark.

● **To measure dry ingredients,** such as flour or sugar, use a dry measuring cup exactly the size you need. Spoon the ingredient into the measuring cup, then level it off with a metal spatula or the flat side of a knife.

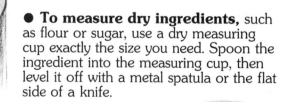

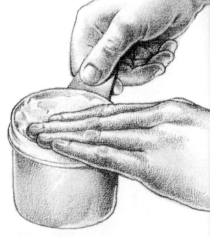

● **To measure brown sugar,** pack it into a dry measuring cup with your hand. Pack it tight enough that when you dump it out, the sugar will hold the shape of the cup.

● **To measure shortening or peanut butter,** pack it into a dry measuring cup with a rubber scraper, pressing out any air pockets.

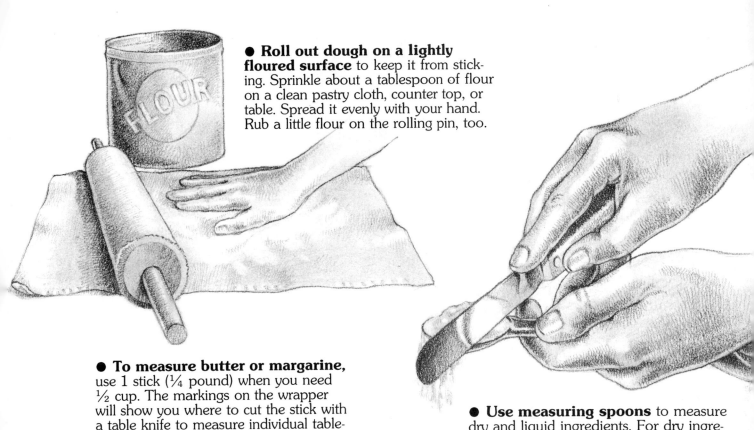

● **Roll out dough on a lightly floured surface** to keep it from sticking. Sprinkle about a tablespoon of flour on a clean pastry cloth, counter top, or table. Spread it evenly with your hand. Rub a little flour on the rolling pin, too.

● **To measure butter or margarine,** use 1 stick (¼ pound) when you need ½ cup. The markings on the wrapper will show you where to cut the stick with a table knife to measure individual tablespoons, ¼ cup, or ⅓ cup.

● **Use measuring spoons** to measure dry and liquid ingredients. For dry ingredients, fill the spoon and level off with a metal spatula or the flat side of a knife. For liquids, fill the spoon to the top.

● **Bake cookies on the middle oven rack** so they bake evenly, using 1 large or 2 small cookie sheets. Use pot holders to handle hot cookie sheets.

● **To grease cookie sheets,** use folded paper toweling or waxed paper to spread the shortening evenly.

● **Preheat the oven** about 10 minutes before putting the cookies in the oven.

● **Check the cookies** at the earliest time they are to be done so they don't overbake. To see if edges are firm, slide a pancake turner under a cookie. If the edges are still doughy, bake longer.

● **Let hot cookie sheets cool** before putting the next batch of dough on them. This will help keep the cookies from spreading out too much.

Everybody-Loves-Chocolate-Chip Cookies

½ cup butter *or* margarine (1 stick) ½ cup shortening 1 cup packed brown sugar ½ cup sugar	● Turn oven to 375°. In a large mixer bowl beat butter or margarine and shortening with electric mixer on medium speed about 30 seconds. Add brown sugar and sugar and beat till fluffy.
2 eggs 1½ teaspoons vanilla	● Add eggs and vanilla. Beat well.
2½ cups all-purpose flour 1 teaspoon baking soda ½ teaspoon salt	● In a medium mixing bowl stir together flour, baking soda, and salt. With mixer on low speed gradually add the flour mixture to the butter mixture, beating till well mixed.
1 6-ounce package (1 cup) semisweet chocolate pieces ½ cup chopped walnuts *or* pecans	● With a wooden spoon stir in chocolate pieces and nuts. Drop by rounded teaspoons about 2 inches apart onto ungreased cookie sheets.
	● Bake in the 375° oven for 8 to 10 minutes or till golden. With a pancake turner lift cookies onto a cooling rack to cool. Makes about 54 cookies.

The cookie no one can improve on—the basic chocolate chip cookie.

The first chocolate chip cookies were made with a chopped up chocolate bar. After people found out how good the cookies were, companies started shaping chocolate into chips like the ones we use in our chocolate chip cookies today.

Neat Wheat Chocolate Chip Cookies: Prepare Everybody-Loves-Chocolate-Chip Cookies as above, *except* substitute 1 cup *whole wheat flour* for 1 cup of the all-purpose flour.

Chocolate Chip Giants: Prepare Everybody-Loves-Chocolate-Chip Cookies as above, *except* put ¼-cup mounds of dough about 4 inches apart on ungreased cookie sheets. Flatten slightly with your fingers. Bake in the 375° oven for 12 to 15 minutes or till golden. Let cookies cool on cookie sheets 1 minute. With a pancake turner lift cookies onto a cooling rack to finish cooling. Makes about 18 large cookies.

A fun, easy way to form *Chocolate Chip Giants* is to drop the dough from an ice cream scoop. Use a scoop that will hold ¼ cup or use one that holds ½ cup and fill it half full.

Giving Cookies

What could be better than a batch of cookies to welcome the new neighbor, say thank you to someone, cheer up a friend, or say you're sorry.
But don't just deliver the cookies on a white paper plate. Present them in a special container. Here are some ideas for fun containers you can make:
● a decorative coffee can or one you decorate yourself with construction paper or adhesive-backed paper.
● a gaily wrapped shoe box.
● a napkin-lined basket.
● a wide-mouthed jar you label "Cookie Jar."

Friend-Chip Cherry Cookies

These flat oatmeal cookies have crispy edges and chewy centers. The chocolate and cherry flavors taste great together!

½ cup butter *or* margarine (1 stick) ½ cup packed brown sugar ¼ cup sugar	● Turn oven to 375°. In a large mixer bowl beat butter or margarine with electric mixer on medium speed till softened (about 30 seconds). Add brown sugar and sugar and beat till fluffy.
1 egg ¼ teaspoon almond extract (optional)	● Add egg and, if desired, almond extract. Beat well.
1 cup all-purpose flour ½ teaspoon baking soda ¼ teaspoon salt	● In a medium mixing bowl stir together flour, baking soda, and salt. With mixer on low speed gradually add the flour mixture to the butter mixture, beating till well mixed.
1 cup quick-cooking rolled oats ½ cup semisweet chocolate pieces ½ cup chopped maraschino cherries ½ cup coconut	● With a wooden spoon stir in oats, chocolate pieces, chopped cherries, and coconut. Drop dough by rounded teaspoons about 2 inches apart onto ungreased cookie sheets.
	● Bake in the 375° oven 8 to 10 minutes or till golden. Let cool on cookie sheets 1 minute. With a pancake turner lift cookies onto cooling rack to finish cooling. Makes about 36 cookies.

Choose-a-Chip Oatmeal Cookies

English Tea Biscuits
(see recipe, page 93)

Choose-a-Chip Oatmeal Cookies

Also pictured on the cover—

Part of the fun of making these crisp oatmeal cookies is that *you* decide what flavor of chips to put in them: chocolate, butterscotch, or peanut butter.

1 cup all-purpose flour ½ cup sugar ½ cup packed brown sugar ½ teaspoon baking soda ½ teaspoon salt	● Turn oven to 375°. In a large mixing bowl stir together the flour, sugar, brown sugar, baking soda, and salt.
½ cup shortening **1** egg **2** tablespoons milk ½ teaspoon vanilla	● Add the shortening, egg, milk, and vanilla. Stir with a wooden spoon till well mixed or mix with your hands.
1½ cups quick-cooking rolled oats **1** 6-ounce package (1 cup) semisweet chocolate pieces, butterscotch pieces, *or* peanut butter-flavored pieces	● Stir in the oats and the chocolate, butterscotch, or peanut butter-flavored pieces. Drop dough by rounded teaspoons about 2 inches apart onto ungreased cookie sheets.
	● Bake in the 375° oven about 10 minutes or till golden. With a pancake turner lift cookies onto a cooling rack to cool. Makes about 48 cookies.

Chocolate Crinkles
(see recipe, page 37)

Peanut Butter Meteors
(see recipe, page 73)

Bump-on-a-Log Cookies
(see recipe, page 46)

Hopscotch Squares
(see recipe, page 51)

Chocolate Oat Wheels
(see recipe, page 34)

Kangaroo Sugar Pockets
(see recipe, page 62)

Citrus Chipsters

½ **cup butter** *or* **margarine** **(1 stick)** ¾ **cup sugar**	● Turn oven to 375°. In a large mixer bowl beat butter or margarine with electric mixer on medium speed till softened (about 30 seconds). Add sugar and beat till fluffy.
1 **egg** 1 **tablespoon finely shredded orange peel** *or* **1 teaspoon finely shredded lemon peel** 2 **tablespoons orange** *or* **lemon juice** 1 **teaspoon vanilla**	● Add egg, finely shredded orange peel or finely shredded lemon peel, orange juice or lemon juice, and vanilla. Beat the mixture well.
1½ **cups all-purpose flour** ½ **teaspoon baking soda** ¼ **teaspoon salt**	● In a medium mixing bowl stir together flour, baking soda, and salt. With mixer on low speed gradually add flour mixture to butter mixture, beating till well mixed.
1 **6-ounce package (1 cup) semisweet chocolate pieces, peanut butter-flavored pieces,** *or* **butterscotch pieces** ½ **cup chopped nuts**	● With a wooden spoon stir in chocolate pieces, peanut butter-flavored pieces, or butterscotch pieces and chopped nuts. Drop dough by rounded teaspoons about 2 inches apart onto ungreased cookie sheets.
	● Bake in the 375° oven for 10 to 12 minutes or till edges are golden. With a pancake turner lift cookies onto a cooling rack. Makes about 36 cookies.

Citrus fruits are tart, juicy fruits such as oranges and lemons. This recipe uses both the peel and the juice of the fruit.

To finely shred citrus peel, rub the fruit over the small shredding holes of a grater. Shred only the colored part of the skin. Stop shredding once you come to the white part.

To get the juice from the fruit, cut the fruit in half crosswise. Then either turn the fruit on a citrus juicer or squeeze it with your hands over a bowl.

Be sure to shred the unpeeled zucchini with the large shredding holes so the zucchini comes out in long, thin pieces.

Martian Cookies

½ cup butter *or* margarine (1 stick) ¾ cup sugar	● Turn oven to 350°. In a large mixer bowl beat butter with electric mixer on medium speed till softened (about 30 seconds). Add sugar and beat till fluffy.
1 egg ½ teaspoon vanilla	● Add egg and vanilla. Beat well.
1½ cups all-purpose flour 1 teaspoon ground cinnamon ½ teaspoon baking soda ½ teaspoon salt	● In a medium mixing bowl stir together flour, cinnamon, baking soda, and salt. With mixer on low speed gradually add flour mixture to butter mixture, beating till well mixed.
1 cup quick-cooking rolled oats 1 cup coarsely shredded unpeeled zucchini 1 cup chopped walnuts *or* pecans ½ cup semisweet chocolate pieces ½ cup butterscotch pieces	● With a wooden spoon stir in quick-cooking rolled oats, shredded zucchini, chopped walnuts or pecans, semisweet chocolate pieces, and butterscotch pieces. Drop dough by rounded teaspoons about 2 inches apart onto ungreased cookie sheets.
	● Bake in the 350° oven for 10 to 12 minutes or till golden. With a pancake turner lift cookies onto a cooling rack to cool. Makes about 48 cookies.

Little green flecks of zucchini and the flavors of cinnamon, chips, and nuts make these soft oatmeal cookies something out of this world.

Peanut Butter Capers

1 cup shortening
1 cup peanut butter
1 cup sugar
1 cup packed brown sugar

● Turn oven to 350°. In a large mixing bowl mix shortening and peanut butter with a wooden spoon. Add sugar and brown sugar. Stir till mixed.

Make fun shapes with this mix-by-hand dough. Anything goes—from unicorns to your initials.

2 eggs
1 teaspoon vanilla

● Add eggs and vanilla. Stir till mixed.

2¼ cups all-purpose flour
2 teaspoons baking soda
¼ teaspoon salt

● In a medium mixing bowl combine flour, baking soda, and salt. Stir into peanut butter mixture till well mixed. Use your hands to mix if you need to.

Here's your chance to play artist. You'll be proud of the way your works of art look and taste.

● Follow the directions at right and below right for shaping the cookies.

1 With your hands, shape the dough into balls and ropes. Place them on an ungreased cookie sheet.

● Bake in the 350° oven for 10 to 12 minutes or till light brown on the edges. Let cool on cookie sheets 1 minute. With a pancake turner lift cookies onto a cooling rack to finish cooling. Makes about 36 large cookies.

1

2

2 With your hands, flatten and push together the pieces of dough to make different shapes.

3 Use little pieces of dough for eyes, noses, buttons, etc. Gently press them into the larger pieces of dough.

3

Cyclops Cookies

½ **cup butter *or* margarine (1 stick)** ½ **cup peanut butter** ½ **cup sugar** ½ **cup packed brown sugar**	● In a large mixer bowl beat butter or margarine and peanut butter with electric mixer on medium speed about 30 seconds. Add the ½ cup sugar and the brown sugar and beat till fluffy.
1 **egg** 2 **tablespoons milk** 1 **teaspoon vanilla**	● Add egg, milk, and vanilla. Beat well.
1¾ **cups all-purpose flour** 1 **teaspoon baking powder** ¼ **teaspoon salt** ⅛ **teaspoon baking soda**	● In a medium mixing bowl stir together flour, baking powder, salt, and baking soda. With mixer on low speed gradually add flour mixture to peanut butter mixture, beating well. If necessary, cover and chill about 1 hour for easier handling.
Sugar	● Turn oven to 375°. Shape dough into 1-inch balls. Roll in additional sugar. Place about 2 inches apart on ungreased cookie sheets.
Milk chocolate kisses	● Bake in the 375° oven 10 to 12 minutes or till edges are firm. Immediately press a chocolate kiss atop each cookie. With a pancake turner lift cookies onto cooling rack. Makes 60.

Top each peanut butter cookie with a chocolate kiss that looks like a great big chocolate chip.

A cyclops is a make-believe giant with one eye in the middle of its forehead. These cookies are named after the cyclops because of the chocolate kiss you put smack in the middle of each cookie right after it comes out of the oven.

Peanut Butter Crisscrosses

1 egg ½ cup sugar ½ cup packed brown sugar	● Turn oven to 350°. In a medium mixing bowl beat egg slightly with a wooden spoon. Beat in sugar and brown sugar with wooden spoon till well combined.	**These peanutty cookies have only 5 ingredients (and no flour!).**
1 cup peanut butter	● Add the peanut butter and stir till the ingredients are well mixed.	
½ cup chopped peanuts	● Stir in the chopped peanuts.	
Sugar	● With your hands, shape dough into 1-inch balls. Place about 2 inches apart on ungreased cookie sheets. With a fork dipped in sugar, press crisscross design in each ball of dough.	**Use a fork to make your mark in each ball of cookie dough. Dip the prongs of the fork in sugar (to keep them from sticking to the dough) and press down on the ball of dough. Then cross the fork over the lines you've already made, and press down again.**
	● Bake in the 350° oven for 10 to 12 minutes or till golden. Let cool on cookie sheets 1 to 2 minutes. With a pancake turner lift cookies onto a cooling rack to finish cooling. Makes about 36 cookies.	

Peanut-Coconut Clouds

¼ cup chunk-style peanut butter	● Turn oven to 325°. Grease cookie sheets with a little shortening. In a small saucepan melt peanut butter over very low heat, stirring constantly. Cool slightly.	**Light-as-a-cloud cookies with a mild peanut butter flavor. Our kid tasters liked them because they were "chewy and crispy."**
2 egg whites ½ teaspoon vanilla Dash salt ⅔ cup sugar	● In a small mixer bowl beat the egg whites, vanilla, and salt with electric mixer on high speed till soft peaks form (tips curl over). Gradually add sugar, beating till stiff peaks form (tips stand straight).	**The trickiest part of this recipe is beating the egg whites and sugar just the right amount of time. Grown-ups may want to lend a hand at this point. The kids can slide the mixture off of a teaspoon onto the cookie sheets (and taste-test the cookies when they're done).**
1 3½-ounce can (1⅓ cups) flaked coconut	● Fold in the coconut and melted peanut butter. Drop by rounded teaspoons about 2 inches apart onto the greased cookie sheets.	
	● Bake in the 325° oven for 15 to 17 minutes or till light golden brown. Let cookies cool on cookie sheets 1 minute. With pancake turner lift cookies onto cooling rack to finish cooling. Makes about 24.	

Peanut Butter Honeys

½ **cup shortening** ½ **cup peanut butter** ½ **cup sugar** ½ **cup honey**	● Turn oven to 350°. Grease cookie sheets with a little shortening. In a large mixing bowl mix ½ cup shortening, the peanut butter, sugar, and honey with a wooden spoon.
1 **egg**	● Beat in egg.
1½ **cups all-purpose flour** ¼ **teaspoon baking soda** ¼ **teaspoon baking powder** ¼ **teaspoon salt**	● In a medium mixing bowl stir together flour, baking soda, baking powder, and salt. Gradually stir flour mixture into peanut butter mixture till well mixed.
	● Drop dough by rounded teaspoons about 2 inches apart onto greased cookie sheets. Bake in the 350° oven about 10 minutes or till cookies are light brown on the bottom. With a pancake turner lift cookies onto a cooling rack to cool. Makes about 42 cookies.

Kids, you can make these cookies with very little help from grown-ups. Just mix the dough with a wooden spoon, drop by spoonfuls onto cookie sheets, and bake.

Peanut Butter Maples: Prepare Peanut Butter Honeys as above, *except* substitute ½ cup *maple-flavored syrup* for the honey.

Peanut Butter M'lassies: Prepare Peanut Butter Honeys as above, *except* substitute ½ cup *molasses* for the honey.

We watched kids as they made these cookies from start to finish. They had fun taking turns measuring the ingredients and stirring the dough. Their love for peanut butter was too great to keep them from sticking a finger into the peanut butter jar for a quick lick. We also found that they made their cookies much bigger than the adults made theirs.

BIG Apple-Peanut Butter Cookies

Apple and oats work together to make the cookies soft and chewy.

¾ **cup peanut butter**
 ¼ **cup butter _or_ margarine**
   (½ stick)
 2 **cups packed brown**
   sugar
	● Turn oven to 350°. In a large mixer bowl beat peanut butter and butter or margarine with electric mixer on medium speed about 30 seconds. Add brown sugar and beat till fluffy.

2 **eggs** 1 **teaspoon vanilla**	● Add eggs and vanilla. Beat well.
1 **cup all-purpose flour** 1 **cup whole wheat flour** 2 **teaspoons baking soda** ¾ **teaspoon salt**	● In a medium mixing bowl stir together all-purpose flour, whole wheat flour, baking soda, and salt. Gradually add flour mixture to peanut butter mixture, beating till well mixed.

1 **cup quick-cooking**
   rolled oats
 1 **medium apple, peeled**
   and chopped (1 cup)
	● With a wooden spoon stir in the quick-cooking rolled oats and the chopped, peeled apple.

	● Put ¼-cup mounds of dough about 4 inches apart on ungreased cookie sheets. Flatten each mound of dough slightly with your fingers.
	● Bake in the 350° oven for 12 to 14 minutes or till edges are firm. Let cookies cool on cookie sheets 1 minute. With a pancake turner lift cookies onto a cooling rack to finish cooling. Makes about 20 large cookies.

For hundreds of years people have told tales about apples. One story says that when an unmarried lady peels an apple and throws the twisted peeling over her shoulder, the peeling will land on the ground in the shape of her husband's initials.

The truth is that apples add flavor and nutrients to the foods you put them in, such as these jumbo peanut butter cookies.

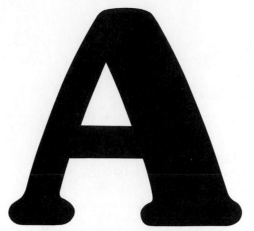

is for Apple Cookies

Like homemade apple pie, these moist cookies are brimming with apples and fill the house with a wonderful aroma as they bake. They're sure to bring a smile to any face.

½ cup butter *or* margarine (1 stick) 1⅓ cups packed brown sugar	● Turn oven to 375°. In a large mixer bowl beat butter or margarine with electric mixer on medium speed till softened (about 30 seconds). Add brown sugar and beat till fluffy.
1 egg ¼ cup milk	● Beat in egg and milk.
2¼ cups all-purpose flour 1 teaspoon baking soda 1 teaspoon ground cinnamon ½ teaspoon salt ½ teaspoon ground nutmeg	● In a medium mixing bowl stir together flour, baking soda, cinnamon, salt, and nutmeg. With mixer on low speed gradually add flour mixture to butter mixture, beating till well mixed.
1 cup chopped walnuts 1 medium apple, chopped (1 cup) 1 cup raisins	● Stir in chopped nuts, chopped apple, and raisins. Drop dough by rounded teaspoons about 2 inches apart onto ungreased cookie sheets.
	● Bake in the 375° oven for 10 to 12 minutes or till the tops of the cookies are brown. With a pancake turner lift the cookies onto a cooling rack to cool. Makes about 42 cookies.

Leave the shiny red peel on the apple that you chop for these cookies. The bits of red peel will dot the baked cookies. Best of all, you'll save yourself the step of peeling the apple.

Banana Bumps

½ cup butter *or* margarine (1 stick)	● Turn oven to 375°. Grease cookie sheets. In large mixer bowl beat butter or margarine with electric mixer on medium speed till softened (about 30 seconds). Add brown sugar and beat till fluffy.
¾ cup packed brown sugar	

Small, soft cookies that keep well because they're so moist.

2 eggs	● Beat in eggs and vanilla. Beat in mashed bananas.
½ teaspoon vanilla	
1 cup mashed bananas (3 medium)	

2 cups all-purpose flour	● In a medium mixing bowl stir together flour, baking powder, cinnamon, baking soda, and salt. With mixer on low speed gradually add flour mixture to banana mixture, beating till well mixed.
1½ teaspoons baking powder	
½ teaspoon ground cinnamon	
¼ teaspoon baking soda	
¼ teaspoon salt	

1 cup raisins	● With a wooden spoon stir in raisins. Drop dough by rounded teaspoons about 2 inches apart onto the greased cookie sheets.

To get 1 cup of mashed bananas, you have to peel and mash about 3 medium-size bananas. Peel a banana, place it in a bowl, and cut it into 3 or 4 pieces. Mash the pieces against the side of the bowl with a fork till no big chunks of banana are left. Spoon the mashed banana into a measuring cup. Do the same with the other bananas till you have 1 level cup.

● Bake in the 375° oven for 10 to 12 minutes or till edges are firm and bottoms are golden. With a pancake turner lift cookies onto a cooling rack to cool. Makes about 50 cookies.

Pumpkin Bumps: Prepare Banana Bumps as above, *except* substitute 1 cup *canned pumpkin* for the mashed bananas and add ⅛ teaspoon *ground cloves* to the flour mixture.

Sweet Potato Bumps: Prepare Banana Bumps as above, *except* substitute 1 cup *mashed cooked sweet potato* for the mashed bananas.

Pineapple Pickups

½ cup butter *or* margarine (1 stick) ¾ cup packed brown sugar	● Turn oven to 375°. In a large mixer bowl beat butter with electric mixer on medium speed till softened. Add brown sugar and beat till fluffy.
1 egg	● Add egg. Beat well.
1¼ cups all-purpose flour ½ teaspoon baking soda ½ teaspoon salt ¼ teaspoon ground ginger	● In a medium mixing bowl stir together flour, baking soda, salt, and ginger. With mixer on low speed gradually add flour mixture to butter mixture, beating well.
1 cup coconut ½ cup well-drained crushed pineapple (juice pack) ½ cup chopped walnuts	● With a wooden spoon stir in coconut, well-drained crushed pineapple, and nuts. Drop dough by rounded teaspoons about 2 inches apart onto ungreased cookie sheets.
	● Bake in the 375° oven for 8 to 10 minutes. Let cool on cookie sheets 30 seconds. With a pancake turner lift cookies onto a cooling rack. Makes about 42.

Some of our young cookie tasters said they usually didn't like coconut, but they loved these soft, chewy cookies.

For this recipe use the crushed pineapple that comes in its own juice rather than the kind that's packed in a sugar syrup. You won't need the extra sweetness from the syrup to make these cookies taste good. Besides, the juice you drain from the pineapple makes a refreshing drink.

Rabbit Rewards

⅔ cup butter *or* margarine ¾ cup packed brown sugar	● Turn oven to 350°. In large mixer bowl beat butter with electric mixer on medium speed till softened. Add brown sugar and beat till fluffy.
2 eggs ⅓ cup honey 1 teaspoon vanilla	● Add the eggs, honey, and vanilla. Beat the mixture well.
2½ cups all-purpose flour 2 teaspoons baking powder ½ teaspoon ground allspice ¼ teaspoon salt	● In a medium mixing bowl stir together flour, baking powder, allspice, and salt. With mixer on low speed gradually add flour mixture to butter mixture, beating till well mixed.
1 cup finely shredded carrots (2 medium) ½ cup sunflower nuts, raisins, *or* chopped nuts	● With a wooden spoon stir in carrots and sunflower nuts, raisins, or nuts. Drop by rounded teaspoons about 2 inches apart onto ungreased cookie sheets.
	● Bake in the 350° oven for 10 to 12 minutes or till golden. Let cookies cool on cookie sheets 1 minute. With a pancake turner lift cookies onto a cooling rack to finish cooling. Makes about 44.

You don't have to be a rabbit to like nibbling on these carrot cookies. The shredded carrots make these honey-sweetened cookies moist and give them their golden color.

An easy way to quarter the apricots is to cut them in half with kitchen shears and then cut each half in half again.

Crowned Rounds

¼ **cup butter *or* margarine (½ stick)** ¾ **cup packed brown sugar**	● Turn oven to 375°. Grease cookie sheets. In a large mixer bowl beat butter or margarine with electric mixer on medium speed till softened (about 30 seconds). Add brown sugar and beat till mixture is well combined.
½ **cup plain yogurt** ½ **teaspoon vanilla**	● Add yogurt and vanilla. Beat well.
1 **cup quick-cooking rolled oats** ¾ **cup all-purpose flour** ¼ **cup toasted wheat germ** ½ **teaspoon baking soda** ½ **teaspoon ground cinnamon**	● In a medium mixing bowl stir together quick-cooking rolled oats, flour, wheat germ, baking soda, and cinnamon. With mixer on low speed gradually add the oat mixture to the butter mixture, beating till well mixed.
Dried apricot halves, quartered	● Drop dough by rounded teaspoons about 2 inches apart onto the greased cookie sheets. Gently press a piece of dried apricot in the top of each cookie.
	● Bake in the 375° oven for 10 to 12 minutes or till the cookies are golden. Let cookies cool on the cookie sheets 1 minute. With a pancake turner lift cookies onto a cooling rack to finish cooling. Makes about 36 cookies.

Thin oatmeal cookies that are crispy on the edges and slightly chewy in the middle. Each cookie is "crowned" with a piece of golden dried apricot.

Be sure to let these cookies cool on the cookie sheets for 1 minute before you remove them. But don't let them cool much longer than that, or they'll crumble when you try to lift them with the pancake turner.

Funny Grahams

⅓ cup butter *or* margarine ⅔ cup packed brown sugar ¼ cup honey 1 teaspoon vanilla	● In a large mixer bowl beat butter or margarine with electric mixer on medium speed till softened (about 30 seconds). Add brown sugar, honey, and vanilla and beat till fluffy.
2 cups whole wheat flour 1 cup all-purpose flour 1 teaspoon baking powder ½ teaspoon baking soda ¼ teaspoon salt ¼ teaspoon ground cinnamon	● In a medium mixing bowl stir together whole wheat flour, all-purpose flour, baking powder, baking soda, salt, and cinnamon. With electric mixer on low speed gradually add *half* of the flour mixture to the butter mixture and beat well.
½ cup milk	● Beat in milk and then the remaining flour mixture till well mixed. Gather the dough into a ball. Cover and chill about 2 hours or till firm enough to roll out.
	● Turn oven to 350°. Grease cookie sheets. Divide dough in half. On a lightly floured surface, roll out half of the dough so it's ⅛ inch to ¼ inch thick. Cut into 2½-inch squares or shapes with a knife or cookie cutters. Transfer shapes to the greased cookie sheets. Prick each shape 4 or 5 times with a fork. Repeat with remaining half of the dough.
	● Bake in the 350° oven for 10 to 12 minutes or till golden. With a pancake turner lift cookies onto a cooling rack to cool. Store in an airtight container. Makes 36 to 48 cookies.

Turn your kitchen table into a graham cracker factory. You can make the square kind of cracker like those you buy in a store or you can make funny shapes. Try making both kinds.

Roll out the chilled dough on a lightly floured surface so the dough is ⅛ to ¼ inch thick.

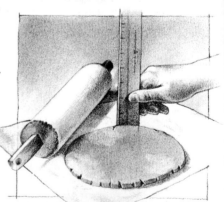

Now you're ready to cut the dough into squares, circles, or any shapes you can think of.

Whole Wheat Humdingers

½ cup butter *or* margarine (1 stick) ¾ cup packed brown sugar	● Turn oven to 350°. Grease cookie sheets. In a large mixer bowl beat butter or margarine with electric mixer on medium speed till softened (about 30 seconds). Add brown sugar and beat till the mixture is fluffy.
1 egg	● Add egg and beat well.
¾ cup whole wheat flour ½ teaspoon baking soda ½ teaspoon salt ¼ teaspoon ground cinnamon ¼ teaspoon ground nutmeg	● In a medium mixing bowl stir together whole wheat flour, baking soda, salt, cinnamon, and nutmeg. With mixer on low speed gradually add flour mixture to butter mixture, beating till well mixed.
1 cup quick-cooking rolled oats ½ cup raisins	● With a wooden spoon, stir in oats and raisins. Drop dough by rounded teaspoons about 2 inches apart onto the greased cookie sheets.
	● Bake in the 350° oven for 8 to 10 minutes or till cookies start to turn brown around edges. Let cookies cool on cookie sheets 1 to 2 minutes. With a pancake turner lift cookies onto a cooling rack to finish cooling. Makes about 32 cookies.

Chewy whole grain cookies that are speckled here and there with raisins—they're a welcome treat in any lunch box or brown-bag lunch.

Take these cookies out of the oven when they start to turn brown on the edges. The longer you leave them in the oven, the crisper they get.

Gorp Cookies

2 eggs
½ cup cooking oil
½ cup honey
½ teaspoon salt
½ teaspoon ground
   cinnamon

● Turn oven to 300°. In a large mixing bowl beat together eggs, cooking oil, honey, salt, and cinnamon with a wooden spoon.

"Gorp" is a quick-energy snack made of dried fruits, oats, nuts, chocolate, and honey. *Gorp Cookies* combine all these things into bite-size mounds for easy eating.

2 cups quick-cooking
   rolled oats
1 cup chopped mixed
   dried fruits
½ cup chopped peanuts
½ cup carob chips *or* semisweet chocolate
   pieces
⅓ cup nonfat dry milk
   powder
⅓ cup toasted wheat germ

● Stir in quick-cooking rolled oats, chopped mixed dried fruits, chopped peanuts, carob chips or chocolate pieces, nonfat dry milk powder, and wheat germ. Drop dough by rounded teaspoons about 2 inches apart onto ungreased cookie sheets.

● Bake in the 300° oven for 12 to 15 minutes or till edges are firm. With a pancake turner lift cookies onto cooling rack to cool. Makes about 54 cookies.

Most of the kids who tasted these cookies didn't know what "gorp" was. When we told them what was in the cookies, they weren't crazy about trying them. But after they did, every one of the kids said, "Yum!"

Drop cookies, such as these, are some of the easiest cookies to make. Get enough dough on a teaspoon so the dough is slightly humped in the spoon. With the back of another spoon, push the dough onto the cookie sheet, leaving 2 inches between each cookie.

Whole Wheat Snickerdoodles

½ cup butter *or* margarine (1 stick) ¾ cup packed brown sugar	● Turn oven to 375°. In a small mixer bowl beat butter or margarine with electric mixer on medium speed till softened (about 30 seconds). Add brown sugar and beat till fluffy.
1 egg 1 teaspoon vanilla	● Add egg and vanilla. Beat well.
1½ cups whole wheat flour ½ teaspoon baking soda ½ teaspoon cream of tartar ¼ teaspoon salt	● In a medium mixing bowl stir together whole wheat flour, baking soda, cream of tartar, and salt. With mixer on low speed gradually add flour mixture to butter mixture, beating till well mixed.
2 tablespoons sugar ½ teaspoon ground cinnamon	● Stir together sugar and cinnamon. Shape the dough into 1-inch balls. Roll the balls in the sugar-cinnamon mixture. Place about 2 inches apart on ungreased cookie sheets. Flatten slightly with the bottom of a drinking glass.
	● Bake in the 375° oven for 8 to 10 minutes or till edges are firm. With a pancake turner lift cookies onto a cooling rack to cool. Makes about 30.

Flat, round cookies with crinkled tops and a sugar-cinnamon coating.
With a fun name like Snickerdoodles, you would expect these cookies to be fun to make. And they are!
After you've shaped the balls of dough and rolled them in the sugar-cinnamon mixture, put them about 2 inches apart on cookie sheets. Now, slightly flatten each ball with the bottom of a drinking glass.

Corn Flake Cookies

Pictured on page 29—

½ cup butter *or* margarine (1 stick) ½ cup sugar ½ cup packed brown sugar	● Turn oven to 375°. In a large mixer bowl beat butter or margarine with electric mixer on medium speed till softened (about 30 seconds). Add sugar and brown sugar and beat till fluffy.
1 egg ½ teaspoon vanilla	● Add egg and vanilla. Beat well.
1¼ cups all-purpose flour ½ teaspoon cream of tartar ½ teaspoon baking soda	● In a medium mixing bowl stir together flour, cream of tartar, and baking soda. With mixer on low speed gradually add flour mixture to butter mixture, beating till well mixed.
1 cup corn flakes	● With a wooden spoon stir in corn flakes. Drop dough by rounded teaspoons about 2 inches apart onto ungreased cookie sheets.
	● Bake in the 375° oven for 8 to 10 minutes or till golden. Let cool on cookie sheets 30 seconds. With a pancake turner lift cookies onto a cooling rack to finish cooling. Makes about 36 cookies.

Usually you eat corn flakes in a bowl with milk. Now see how you like them in these chewy cookies.

Wheat, oat, bran, or four-grain cereal flakes work just as well as corn flakes in these cookies. All of these unsweetened breakfast cereals help make the cookies crisp on the outside and chewy on the inside.

Nut-Cracker Sweets

Pictured on page 29—

36 graham cracker squares	● Turn oven to 350°. To keep the cookies from sticking, cover 2 cookie sheets with foil. Break graham crackers on perforated lines. Place crackers, side by side, on the foil-covered cookie sheets.
½ cup butter *or* margarine (1 stick) ½ cup packed brown sugar	● In a saucepan melt butter or margarine. Stir in brown sugar till well combined. Drizzle atop crackers.
1 cup chopped pecans	● Sprinkle with chopped pecans.
	● Bake in the 350° oven for 8 to 10 minutes. Cool on cookie sheets on a cooling rack. Store in a tightly covered container. Makes 72.

Not many kids will turn down a graham cracker. Here's a fun way to make them even more of a treat.
   These cracker-cookies stay crisp for days in a tightly covered container.

1 Roll the chilled cookie dough between your hands to make 1-inch balls. (As you can see, that's about as big across as a bottle cap.)

2 Dip the balls of dough in slightly beaten egg white. Then roll them in finely chopped nuts.

Jam Thumbprints

Even if you think you're "all thumbs," you can make *Jam Thumbprints*. Just roll 'em, poke 'em, and fill 'em.

⅔ cup butter *or* margarine ⅓ cup sugar ¼ teaspoon salt	● In a large mixer bowl beat butter or margarine with electric mixer on medium speed till softened (about 30 seconds). Add sugar and salt and beat till fluffy.
2 egg yolks 1 teaspoon vanilla	● Add egg yolks and vanilla. Beat well.
1½ cups all-purpose flour	● With mixer on low speed gradually add flour to butter mixture, beating till well mixed. Cover and chill in the refrigerator about 1 hour or till firm enough to handle.
1 slightly beaten egg white ¾ cup finely chopped walnuts	● Turn oven to 350°. Shape dough into 1-inch balls. Roll in egg white, then nuts. Place 2 inches apart on ungreased cookie sheets. Press down the center of each ball with your thumb.
⅓ cup of your favorite jam *or* jelly	● Bake in the 350° oven for 15 to 17 minutes or till light brown on bottom. With a pancake turner lift cookies onto a cooling rack to cool. Just before serving, fill centers with jam or jelly. Makes about 36 cookies.

3 Put the nut-coated balls on cookie sheets. Press your thumb in the center of each ball to make a hole.

4 After you bake the cookies, plug up the hole with a dab of your favorite jam or jelly.

Amazin' Raisin-Catsup Cookies

½ cup butter *or* margarine (1 stick) ¾ cup packed brown sugar	● Turn oven to 375°. Grease cookie sheets with a little shortening. In a large mixer bowl beat butter or margarine with electric mixer on medium speed till softened (about 30 seconds). Add brown sugar and beat till fluffy.	**You'd never know catsup is in these moist little cookies. That's what gives them their gentle spice and rosy blush.**
1 egg ½ teaspoon vanilla 2 tablespoons catsup	● Beat in egg and vanilla. Add the catsup and beat well.	
1⅓ cups all-purpose flour ¼ teaspoon baking soda	● In a medium mixing bowl stir together flour and baking soda. With mixer on low speed gradually add flour mixture to butter mixture, beating till well mixed.	
¾ cup raisins	● With a wooden spoon stir in raisins. Drop dough by rounded teaspoons about 2 inches apart onto the greased cookie sheets.	
Powdered Sugar Icing (optional)	● Bake in the 375° oven for 10 to 12 minutes or till golden. With a pancake turner lift cookies onto a cooling rack. When cool, lightly spread cookies with Powdered Sugar Icing if desired. Makes about 40 cookies.	**If you choose to frost the cookies with icing, be sure to make it thin enough to spread but not so thin it pours.** **The best way to make the icing is to put the powdered sugar in a bowl and add the milk a teaspoon at a time, stirring with a fork till the icing is the right thickness.**
	Powdered Sugar Icing: In a small mixing bowl use a fork to stir together 1 cup sifted *powdered sugar* and enough *milk* (3 to 4 teaspoons) to make an icing that is thin enough to spread.	

Does it seem flaky to put corn flakes in cookies? Is making cookies out of graham crackers kind of square? Do you think that making cookies with catsup doesn't cut the mustard? These cookies made from some of your favorite foods may sound strange, but they're sure to leave a good taste in your mouth.

Corn Flake Cookies
(see recipe, page 26)

Potato Chip Munchies
(see recipe, page 31)

**Amazin' Raisin-
Catsup Cookies**

**Sparkling Lemonade
Cookies**
(see recipe, page 30)

Jam Thumprints
(see recipe, page 27)

Nut-Cracker Sweets
(see recipe, page 26)

Sparkling Lemonade Cookies

Pictured on page 29—

1 cup butter *or* margarine (2 sticks) 1 cup sugar	● Turn oven to 375°. In a large mixer bowl beat butter or margarine with electric mixer on medium speed till softened (about 30 seconds). Add sugar and beat till fluffy.
2 eggs	● Beat in eggs.
3 cups all-purpose flour 1 teaspoon baking soda	● In a medium mixing bowl stir together flour and baking soda. With electric mixer on low speed gradually add *half* of the flour mixture to the butter mixture and beat the mixture well.
1 6-ounce can frozen lemonade concentrate, thawed (⅔ cup)	● Beat in ½ *cup* of the lemonade concentrate and then the remaining flour mixture till well mixed. Drop dough by rounded teaspoons about 2 inches apart onto ungreased cookie sheets.
Sugar	● Bake in the 375° oven for 10 to 12 minutes or till light brown on bottom. With a pancake turner lift cookies onto a cooling rack. Cool 10 minutes. Lightly brush cookies with remaining lemonade concentrate. Sprinkle with a little sugar. Makes about 60 cookies.

Refreshing softies with tart and sugary tops. You'll need one can of frozen lemonade for these cookies—some to mix into the cookie dough and some to brush on the cookies after they've baked and cooled.

Use a pastry brush (if you don't have one, use a clean finger) to brush the cooled cookies with lemonade concentrate.

Crush the potato chips before you add them. Put some chips in a plastic bag, press out most of the air, and close the end of the bag. Now tap the chips with your fist or press with your hands till they're crushed into tiny pieces. Empty them into a measuring cup and do the same with the rest of the chips till you have 1 cup of crushed chips.

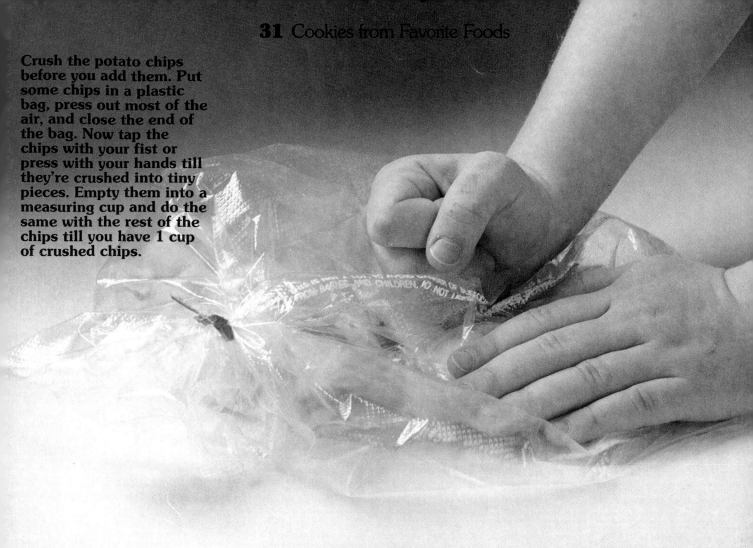

Potato Chip Munchies

Pictured on page 29—

1 cup butter *or* margarine (2 sticks) ½ cup sugar 1 teaspoon vanilla	● Turn oven to 350°. In a large mixer bowl beat butter or margarine with electric mixer on medium speed till softened (about 30 seconds). Add the ½ cup sugar and vanilla and beat till fluffy.	**These cookies really have potato chips in them. And they crunch and taste like potato chips, too.**
1¾ cups all-purpose flour 1 cup crushed potato chips (5 cups uncrushed) Sugar	● With mixer on low speed gradually add flour and potato chips, beating till well mixed. Drop by rounded teaspoons about 2 inches apart onto ungreased cookie sheets. Flatten the dough with a fork that has been dipped in sugar.	
	● Bake in the 350° oven for 12 to 15 minutes or till golden. With a pancake turner lift the cookies onto a cooling rack to cool. Makes about 36 cookies.	

Each cookie has a cherry hiding under the rich chocolate frosting.

To make the frosting the right thickness, use only real (not imitation) semisweet chocolate pieces.

Buried Cherry Cookies

1

½ cup butter *or* margarine (1 stick) 1 cup sugar	● Turn oven to 350°. In a large mixer bowl beat butter or margarine with electric mixer on medium speed till softened (about 30 seconds). Add sugar and beat till mixture is fluffy.
1 egg 1½ teaspoons vanilla	● Add egg and vanilla. Beat well.
1½ cups all-purpose flour ½ cup unsweetened cocoa powder ¼ teaspoon baking soda ¼ teaspoon baking powder ¼ teaspoon salt	● In a medium mixing bowl stir together flour, cocoa powder, baking soda, baking powder, and salt. With mixer on low speed gradually add flour mixture to butter mixture, beating till well mixed.
	● Shape dough into 1-inch balls. Place about 2 inches apart on ungreased cookie sheets. Press down center of each ball with your thumb.
1 10-ounce jar maraschino cherries (about 48)	● Drain cherries, reserving juice. Place a cherry in the center of each cookie.
1 6-ounce package (1 cup) semisweet chocolate pieces (*not* imitation) ½ cup Eagle Brand sweetened condensed milk	● For frosting, in a small saucepan combine chocolate and condensed milk. Cook and stir over low heat till chocolate is melted. Stir in *4 teaspoons* reserved cherry juice. Spoon 1 teaspoon frosting over each cherry, spreading to cover cherry. (Frosting may be thinned with additional cherry juice if necessary.)
	● Bake in the 350° oven about 10 minutes or till edges are firm. With a pancake turner lift cookies onto a cooling rack to cool. Makes about 48 cookies.

Bury the cherries by following these fun steps:

1 Press down the center of each ball of dough with your thumb.

2 Drain the juice from the maraschino cherries.

3 Put a maraschino cherry in each thumbprint.

4 Make a frosting using some of the cherry juice. Spread over each cherry *before* baking the cookies.

Chocolate Oat Wheels

Pictured on page 9—

1 cup sugar ½ cup shortening	● Turn oven to 350°. In a large mixer bowl beat together the 1 cup sugar and the shortening with electric mixer on medium speed till fluffy.
2 squares (2 ounces) un-sweetened chocolate *or* 2 envelopes (2 ounces) premelted unsweetened chocolate product 1 egg 2 tablespoons water 1½ teaspoons vanilla	● If using squares of chocolate, in a small saucepan melt chocolate squares over low heat, stirring often. Remove from heat and let cool. 　To the shortening mixture add the melted and cooled chocolate or the pre-melted chocolate product, the egg, water, and vanilla. Beat well.
1 cup all-purpose flour ½ teaspoon baking soda ½ teaspoon salt	● In a medium mixing bowl stir together flour, baking soda, and salt. With electric mixer on low speed gradually add the flour mixture to the chocolate mixture, beating till well mixed.
1 cup quick-cooking rolled oats ½ cup chopped pecans	● With a wooden spoon stir in the oats and chopped pecans.
Sugar	● Drop dough by rounded teaspoons about 2 inches apart onto ungreased cookie sheets. Flatten the dough with the bottom of a drinking glass that has been dipped in sugar.
	● Bake in the 350° oven for 10 to 12 minutes or till edges of cookies are firm. With a pancake turner lift the cookies onto a cooling rack to cool. Makes about 48 cookies.

When you hear the word wheels, what do you think of? Wagon wheels, pin-wheels, steering wheels, Ferris wheels, race car wheels? Here's a new one to add to the list—*Chocolate Oat Wheels*. These crisp round cookies will roll right into your mouth.

If you like your cookies with slightly chewy cen-ters, don't flatten them with a sugared glass. Just drop the dough onto the cookie sheets and bake.

Cocoa-Mint Yo-Yos

½ cup butter *or* margarine
   (1 stick)
1 cup sugar
1 egg

● Turn oven to 400°. Grease cookie sheets. In a large mixer bowl beat the ½ cup butter or margarine with electric mixer on medium speed till softened (about 30 seconds). Add sugar and beat till fluffy. Beat in egg.

Spread mint-flavored filling between 2 chocolate cookies and you've made the best tasting yo-yo you'll ever eat.

2 cups all-purpose flour
½ cup unsweetened cocoa
   powder
½ teaspoon baking soda
½ teaspoon baking powder
¼ teaspoon salt

● In a medium mixing bowl stir together flour, cocoa powder, baking soda, baking powder, and salt. With mixer on low speed add *half* of the flour mixture to the butter mixture and beat well.

If you don't have buttermilk, you can make sour milk with regular milk and lemon juice or vinegar. To make 1⅓ cups sour milk, put 4 teaspoons *vinegar or lemon juice* in a 2-cup liquid measuring cup. Then add enough *milk* to make 1⅓ cups.

1⅓ cups buttermilk *or* sour
   milk

● Beat in the buttermilk or sour milk and then the remaining flour mixture till well mixed.

Mint Filling:
3 cups sifted powdered
   sugar
6 tablespoons butter *or*
   margarine, softened
2 tablespoons milk
¼ teaspoon peppermint
   extract
3 *or* 4 drops green food
   coloring

In a small mixer bowl combine powdered sugar, 6 tablespoons softened butter or margarine, 2 tablespoons milk, the peppermint extract, and food coloring. Beat on low speed till smooth. If necessary, stir in additional milk till filling is easy to spread.

● Drop dough by rounded teaspoons about 3 inches apart onto the greased cookie sheets. Bake in the 400° oven for 7 to 9 minutes or till edges are firm and cookies are no longer shiny. With a pancake turner lift cookies onto a cooling rack to cool.

● Make Mint Filling (see box at left).

● To assemble, spread a rounded teaspoon of the Mint Filling on the flat side of *half* of the cooled cookies. Place remaining cookies, rounded side up, atop Mint Filling. Makes about 36 cookies.

Calico Critters

½ cup butter *or* margarine (1 stick)	● Turn oven to 375°. In a large mixer bowl beat butter with electric mixer till softened. Add sugar and brown sugar and beat till fluffy.
½ cup sugar	
½ cup packed brown sugar	

1 egg	● Beat in egg and vanilla. Stir in sour cream.
1 teaspoon vanilla	
½ cup dairy sour cream	

1¾ cups all-purpose flour	● In a medium mixing bowl stir together flour, baking soda, and salt. With mixer on low speed gradually add flour mixture to butter mixture, beating till well mixed.
½ teaspoon baking soda	
½ teaspoon salt	

1 envelope (1 ounce) premelted unsweetened chocolate product *or* 1 square (1 ounce) un- sweetened chocolate, melted and cooled	● Divide dough in half. Stir chocolate into *one* half. (If dough is sticky, cover and chill in the refrigerator about 30 minutes.) To form critters, drop plain dough and chocolate dough by rounded teaspoons onto ungreased cookie sheets so that the mounds of dough for each critter just touch. Keep critters about 3 inches apart.

Assorted nuts	● Decorate with assorted nuts or addi- tional dough.

● Bake in the 375° oven about 12 min- utes or till plain part of cookie is golden. With a pancake turner lift cookies onto a cooling rack to cool. Makes about 20.

Try making some of the characters you see on this page or make up your own critters. Before you bake them, give them eyes, noses, feelers, feet, and tails with nuts or little blobs of dough. Make some critters chocolate, some vanilla, and some two-toned.

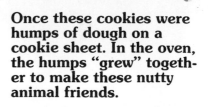

Once these cookies were humps of dough on a cookie sheet. In the oven, the humps "grew" togeth- er to make these nutty animal friends.

Chocolate Crinkles

Pictured on page 8—

4 squares (4 ounces) un-
  sweetened chocolate *or*
  4 envelopes (4 ounces)
  premelted unsweetened
  chocolate product
3 beaten eggs
1½ cups sugar
½ cup cooking oil
2 teaspoons vanilla

● If using squares of chocolate, in a small saucepan melt chocolate squares over low heat, stirring often. Remove from heat and let cool.
  In a large mixing bowl beat together eggs, sugar, cooking oil, vanilla, and melted and cooled chocolate or premelted chocolate product with a wooden spoon.

Don't be surprised when you take the cookies out of the oven and the powdered sugar coating is "crinkled" or cracked on top. Inside, you'll find a chewy chocolate center.

2 cups all-purpose flour
2 teaspoons baking
  powder

● In a medium mixing bowl stir together flour and baking powder. Gradually add to chocolate mixture, stirring with wooden spoon till well mixed. Cover and chill in the refrigerator for 1 to 2 hours or till firm enough to handle.

¼ cup sifted powdered
  sugar

● Turn oven to 375°. With your hands, shape dough into 1-inch balls. Place powdered sugar in a small mixing bowl. Roll the balls in the powdered sugar. Place about 2 inches apart on ungreased cookie sheets.

● Bake in the 375° oven for 10 to 12 minutes or till edges are firm. With a pancake turner lift cookies onto a cooling rack to cool. If desired, sprinkle with additional powdered sugar. Makes about 48 cookies.

Chilling stiffens the dough so it's easy to roll into 1-inch balls.

Sifting Powdered Sugar

The powdered sugar that you roll the balls of dough in should be sifted to get rid of any clumps. One way to do this is to sift it in a flour sifter over a bowl or waxed paper. Another way is to place a metal sieve over a bowl, add the powdered sugar, and stir it around with a spoon till all the powdered sugar has gone through the little holes of the sieve.

Chocolate and Vanilla Checkers

1 cup butter *or* margarine (2 sticks) ⅓ cup sugar 1 teaspoon vanilla	● Turn oven to 325°. In a large mixer bowl beat butter or margarine with electric mixer on medium speed till softened (about 30 seconds). Add sugar and vanilla and beat till fluffy.
2½ cups all-purpose flour	● With mixer on low speed gradually add flour to butter mixture, beating till well mixed.
2 tablespoons unsweetened cocoa powder	● Divide dough in half. With your hands, knead cocoa powder into one half of the dough.

● On a lightly floured pastry cloth, bread board, table, or counter top roll out the vanilla dough with a rolling pin so it's ½ inch thick. Cut out 1¼-inch rounds with a cookie cutter that has been dipped in flour to keep it from sticking. Repeat rolling and cutting out rounds with the chocolate dough.

● Place the rounds of vanilla and chocolate dough about 1 inch apart on ungreased cookie sheets. If desired, with the prongs of a fork, gently make indentations around the top edge of the cookies to look like the ridges on checkers.

● Bake in the 325° oven for 20 to 25 minutes or till edges of vanilla cookies are golden and chocolate cookies are light brown on the bottom when lifted with a pancake turner. With pancake turner lift cookies onto a cooling rack to cool. Makes about 48 cookies.

Play a game of these checkers and you can eat the checkers you jump! Before you start the game, cover the checkerboard with clear plastic wrap so you don't get crumbs on the board.

To make the cookies look more like checkers, press fork prongs around the top of each round of dough to form ridges.

Knuckle Sandwiches

How would you like a *Knuckle Sandwich* in the mouth? Each one gives you **4 bites** of tender cookie filled with apple butter or jam (and nuts if you like) and sprinkled with sugar and cinnamon.

6 tablespoons butter *or* margarine **¼** cup sugar **¼** cup packed brown sugar	● In a large mixer bowl beat butter or margarine with electric mixer on medium speed till softened (about 30 seconds). Add the ¼ cup sugar and brown sugar and beat till fluffy.
1 egg **½** teaspoon vanilla	● Add egg and vanilla. Beat well.
1½ cups all-purpose flour **½** teaspoon baking powder **¼** teaspoon salt	● Combine flour, baking powder, and salt. Gradually add flour mixture to butter mixture, beating well. Cover; chill 1 to 2 hours or till firm enough to roll out.
	● Turn oven to 375°. On a lightly floured surface roll out dough into a 12-inch square. Cut into 3-inch squares.
⅓ cup apple butter *or* your favorite jam **3** tablespoons chopped walnuts *or* pecans (optional)	● Spread about 1 teaspoon of the apple butter or jam down the middle of each square. If desired, sprinkle about ½ teaspoon chopped nuts over apple butter or jam on each square.
	● Fold one edge of the dough over the filling. Fold over the other edge. With a pancake turner carefully lift cookies onto ungreased cookie sheets.
1 tablespoon sugar **¼** teaspoon ground cinnamon	● With a knife, make 3 cuts halfway through dough on one long side of each cookie. Bend slightly to separate cuts. Combine the 1 tablespoon sugar and the cinnamon; sprinkle over cookies.
	● Bake in the 375° oven for 8 to 10 minutes or till golden. With pancake turner lift the cookies onto a cooling rack to cool. Makes 16 cookies.

You may have seen pastries in the bakery that look like these cookies. The pastries often are called "bear claws" and are quite a bit larger than these cookie-jar treats. As the ruler at right shows you, our cookies are only about three inches long.

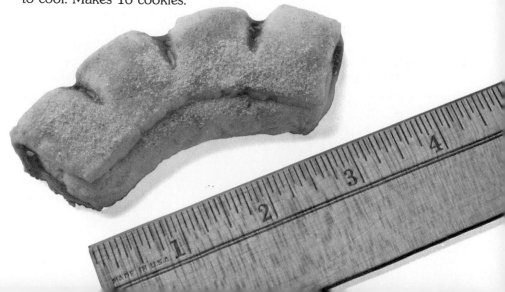

-and- Eat Cookies

¾ cup butter *or* margarine (1½ sticks) ¾ cup sugar	● In a large mixer bowl beat butter or margarine with electric mixer on medium speed till softened (about 30 seconds). Add the ¾ cup sugar and beat till fluffy.
1 egg ½ teaspoon almond extract	● Add egg and almond extract. Beat the mixture well.
2 cups all-purpose flour ¼ teaspoon baking powder ¼ teaspoon salt	● Combine flour, baking powder, and salt. Gradually add flour mixture to butter mixture, beating well. Divide dough in half. Wrap each half in clear plastic wrap. Chill in the refrigerator 30 minutes or till firm enough to handle.
	● Turn oven to 375°. Work with half of the dough at a time. For each cookie, use 2 tablespoons dough. On a lightly floured surface roll each piece of dough into a 10-inch rope. On ungreased cookie sheets shape ropes into letters.
Milk 2 to 4 tablespoons sugar *or* colored sugar	● Brush lightly with milk and sprinkle with the 2 to 4 tablespoons sugar or colored sugar.
	● Bake in the 375° oven about 10 minutes or till golden. With a pancake turner lift cookies onto a cooling rack to cool. Makes about 24 cookies.

Make ropes of dough into different letters, and bake. Then put them together to make words. See how many different words you can make using the same letters.

For fun party favors, make the first letter of your guests' names and place on the table where they are to sit.

With a pastry brush or clean finger, lightly brush dough with milk. Sprinkle with sugar and bake.

Try this pizza for dessert! It's easy enough for a quick treat but special enough to make for a birthday party.

Rocky Road Pizza

1 cup butter *or* margarine (2 sticks) ½ cup sugar ½ cup packed brown sugar	● Turn oven to 375°. In a large mixer bowl beat butter or margarine with electric mixer on medium speed till softened (about 30 seconds). Add sugar and brown sugar and beat till fluffy.
1 egg 1 teaspoon vanilla 1¾ cups all-purpose flour	● Add egg and vanilla. Beat well. With mixer on low speed gradually beat in flour. Spread dough evenly in an ungreased 14-inch pizza pan.
1 cup peanuts 1 cup tiny marshmallows 1 6-ounce package (1 cup) semisweet chocolate pieces	● Bake in the 375° oven about 12 minutes or till golden. Sprinkle peanuts, marshmallows, and semisweet chocolate pieces atop hot crust. (If you like, make each section of the pizza different by sprinkling different combinations on each section.)

● Return pizza to the 375° oven. Bake 6 to 8 minutes more or till marshmallows are golden. Cool in pan on cooling rack.

● To serve pizza, cut into wedges or squares with a pizza cutter or sharp knife. Makes about 32 pieces.

Spread dough evenly in pizza pan with a metal spatula or knife. Bake.

Scatter peanuts, tiny marshmallows, and chocolate chips over the hot crust and finish baking.

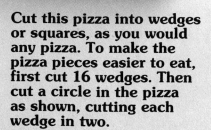

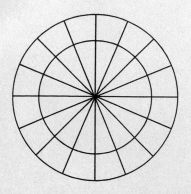

Cut this pizza into wedges or squares, as you would any pizza. To make the pizza pieces easier to eat, first cut 16 wedges. Then cut a circle in the pizza as shown, cutting each wedge in two.

These tasty turtles are a snap to shape. They have pecan feet, candy-stuffed cookie bodies, and chocolate shells.

Shape the dough into 1-inch balls. Press a piece of candy into each ball and mold the dough around it.

For feet, arrange on ungreased cookie sheets groups of 4 pecan halves so their ends touch. Space groups 2 inches apart.

Put a ball of candy-stuffed dough atop each group of pecan halves.

Snapping Turtles

6 tablespoons butter *or* margarine ⅓ cup shortening ⅔ cup packed brown sugar	● In a large mixer bowl beat butter or margarine and shortening with electric mixer on medium speed 30 seconds. Add brown sugar and beat till fluffy.
1 egg 1 teaspoon vanilla	● Add egg and vanilla. Beat well.
1¾ cups all-purpose flour ½ teaspoon baking soda ½ teaspoon baking powder ¼ teaspoon salt	● Stir together flour, baking soda, baking powder, and salt. Gradually add flour mixture to butter mixture, beating well. Cover and chill in the refrigerator about 1 hour or till firm enough to handle.
Pecan halves Assorted candy*	● Turn oven to 325°. Follow directions above for shaping turtles.
	● Bake in the 325° oven for 15 to 20 minutes. Let cool on cookie sheets 1 minute. With a pancake turner lift cookies onto a cooling rack to finish cooling.
1 6-ounce package (1 cup) semisweet chocolate pieces	● In small saucepan melt chocolate pieces over low heat. Spread atop cookies. Store in refrigerator. Makes 48.

*Note: Candies that work best are ½-inch pieces of chocolate-covered nougat bars with peanuts or caramel, candy-coated milk chocolate-covered peanuts, and chocolate-coated caramel candies.

Cut-It-Out Cookies

1 cup butter *or* margarine (2 sticks) 1 cup sugar	● In a large mixer bowl beat butter or margarine with electric mixer on medium speed till softened (about 30 seconds). Add sugar and beat till fluffy.
2 tablespoons milk 1 teaspoon vanilla	● Add milk and vanilla. Beat well.
2½ cups all-purpose flour	● Gradually beat in flour till well mixed. Mix in last part of flour with a wooden spoon or with your hands.
	● Divide dough into 4 parts. Wrap each part in clear plastic wrap. Chill in refrigerator for 1 to 2 hours or till firm enough to roll out.
	● Turn oven to 375°. Remove one piece of dough from refrigerator and unwrap. On a lightly floured surface roll out dough so it's ¼ inch thick. Use floured cookie cutters to cut out shapes. Place on ungreased cookie sheet. Decorate as desired. Repeat with remaining dough.
	● Bake in the 375° oven about 8 minutes or till edges are light brown. Let cool on cookie sheets 1 minute. With a pancake turner lift cookies onto a cooling rack. Makes 36 to 48 cookies.

Also pictured on the cover—

You'll have an easy time rolling and cutting out this sugar-cookie dough because it handles so well. And you'll find that the shapes you can make are endless if you just "think fun."

Dip your cookie cutters into flour before cutting so they won't stick to the dough. Reroll the scraps of dough so you can cut out more shapes.

Put the decorations for your cookies in the cups of a muffin pan so they'll be handy.

For paint, mix food coloring and water. Cotton swabs make great artist's brushes, and you can use both ends to paint.

Check the cupboard to see what you can use to decorate cookies. Red cinnamon candies and miniature chocolate pieces make good eyes. Press cereal flakes into dough for feathers or hair. Use round toasted oat cereal for circles. Mix cocoa powder and water to draw brown lines with a toothpick.

Put kitchen utensils to work. Squeeze dough through a garlic press for hair, fur, spaghetti, or grass. And turn a jar lid into a cookie cutter.

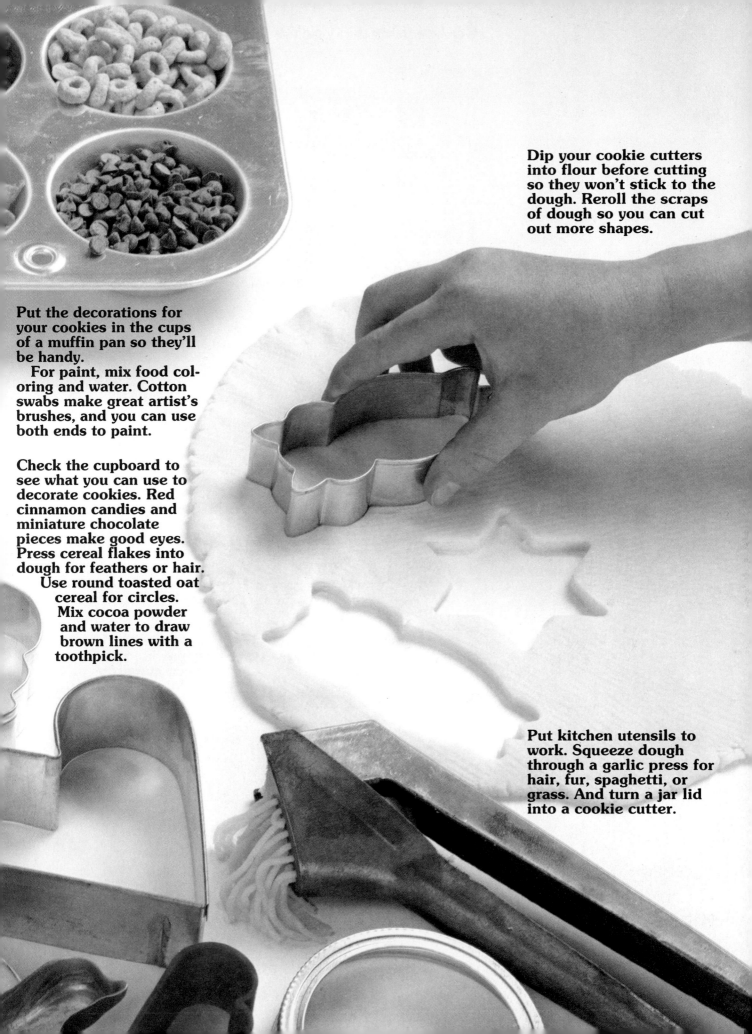

Bump-on-a-Log Cookies

Pictured on page 9—

½ cup butter *or* margarine (1 stick) ⅔ cup sugar ¼ cup unsweetened cocoa powder 1 egg 1 teaspoon vanilla	● In a large mixer bowl beat butter or margarine with electric mixer on medium speed till softened (about 30 seconds). Add sugar, cocoa powder, egg, and vanilla and beat till fluffy.	**Don't sit there like a bump on a log. Join in the fun shaping chocolate cookie logs and decorating them with candy "bumps."**
¼ cup water 2 cups all-purpose flour	● With mixer on low speed beat in water. Gradually add flour, beating till well mixed. If necessary, cover and chill dough in the refrigerator about 2 hours or till firm enough to handle.	
	● Turn oven to 350°. Divide dough into 12 equal parts. On a lightly floured surface roll each part of the dough into a 12-inch rope. With a table knife cut ropes into 3-inch logs.	
Small gumdrops, halved, *and/or* candy-coated milk chocolate-covered peanuts	● Place logs about 1 inch apart on ungreased cookie sheets. Lightly press 3 or 4 candies atop each log.	**Make cookie "stoplights" by putting red, yellow, and green gumdrops on logs of dough.**
	● Bake in the 350° oven for 12 to 15 minutes or till the cookies are no longer glossy. With a pancake turner lift the cookies onto a cooling rack to cool. Makes about 48 cookies.	

This dough is so much fun to play with, you may forget it's cookie dough. Make your masterpieces right on a cookie sheet. You'll make less mess and you won't have to move them.

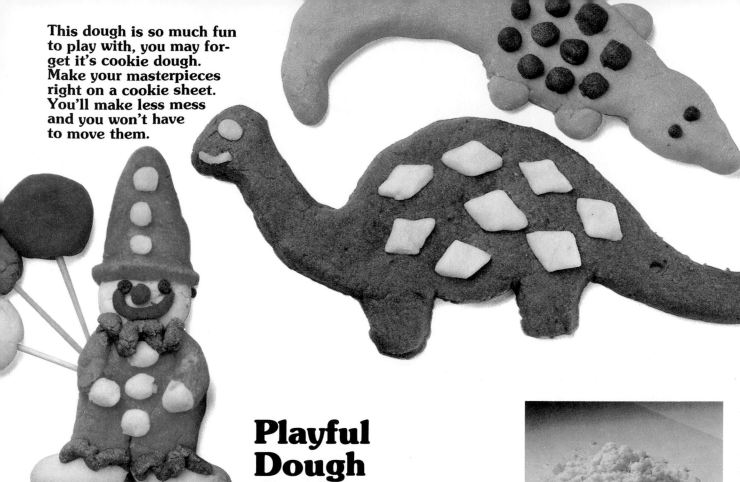

Playful Dough Cookies

⅔ cup butter *or* margarine **⅓ cup sugar**	● Turn oven to 300°. In a large mixer bowl beat butter or margarine with electric mixer on medium speed till softened (about 30 seconds). Add sugar and beat till the mixture is fluffy.
½ teaspoon almond extract	● Beat in almond extract.
1⅔ cups all-purpose flour	● With mixer on low speed gradually add flour, beating till mixture resembles coarse crumbs. Divide mixture into several parts, depending on how many different colors you want.
Food coloring	● Add food coloring to each part, kneading with your hands till the dough is smooth. Form the dough into shapes that are about ¾ inch thick. Place cookies about 1 inch apart on ungreased cookie sheets.
	● Bake in the 300° oven for 20 to 25 minutes or till edges are firm but bottoms are not brown. With a pancake turner lift cookies onto a cooling rack to cool. Makes about 2 cups of dough.

After you mix in the flour, this dough will be fairly crumbly.

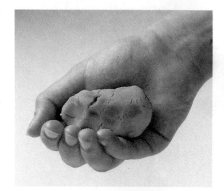

But when you knead in the food coloring, the dough will be smooth and easy to shape.

Waffle Cookies

They look and taste like crisp little waffles.

	● Using a pastry brush, lightly brush the grid surface of a waffle baker with shortening or cooking oil. Preheat the waffle baker on medium heat.
¼ cup butter *or* margarine (½ stick) ¼ cup sugar	● In a small mixer bowl beat butter or margarine with electric mixer on medium speed till softened (about 30 seconds). Add sugar and beat till fluffy.
1 egg 1 tablespoon maple-flavored syrup	● Add egg and maple-flavored syrup. Beat well.
⅔ cup all-purpose flour ½ teaspoon baking powder ½ teaspoon ground cinnamon Dash salt	● In a medium mixing bowl stir together flour, baking powder, cinnamon, and salt. With mixer on low speed gradually add the flour mixture to the butter mixture, beating till well mixed.
Powdered sugar	● Drop by rounded teaspoons about 2 inches apart onto the hot greased grid of the waffle baker. Close lid and bake for 1 to 2 minutes or till firm. Use a fork to lift cookies onto a cooling rack to cool. Sprinkle with powdered sugar. Makes about 20 cookies.

To keep the cookies from sticking, brush the waffle baker grid with shortening. Close the lid and set at medium heat. It's ready when water sprinkled on the grid hops across the surface.

Chocolate Waffle Cookies: Prepare Waffle Cookies as above, *except* add 2 tablespoons *unsweetened cocoa powder* to the flour mixture, substitute 1 tablespoon *milk* for the maple-flavored syrup, and add 1 teaspoon *vanilla*.

Drop spoonfuls of batter 2 inches apart so they don't spread into one another as they bake.

Gingerbread Doghouse

1 cup butter *or* margarine (2 sticks) 1 cup sugar	● In a large mixer bowl beat butter with electric mixer on medium speed till softened. Add sugar and beat till fluffy.
1 egg ½ cup molasses 2 tablespoons lemon juice	● Add egg, molasses, and lemon juice. Beat the mixture well.
3 cups all-purpose flour 1 cup whole wheat flour 1½ teaspoons ground ginger 1½ teaspoons ground allspice 1 teaspoon baking soda ½ teaspoon salt	● Combine all-purpose flour, whole wheat flour, ginger, allspice, baking soda, and salt. Gradually add to butter mixture, beating well. Divide dough in half. Wrap each in clear plastic wrap. Chill 3 hours or till firm enough to roll out.
	● To make patterns, cut out of cardboard the 6 pieces as shown. Turn oven to 375°. Grease cookie sheets. Roll out dough, one half at a time, on lightly floured surface so it's ¼ inch thick. Using the patterns and a knife, cut out the 6 pieces of dough. Place on greased cookie sheets. With a knife mark side pieces (B, C, D, E) for a log-cabin effect.
	● Bake in the 375° oven for 10 to 12 minutes. Let cool on cookie sheets 1 minute. Remove to cooling rack.
1 can vanilla frosting Assorted candies	● Assemble and decorate with frosting and candies, following directions at right.

Assembling: **Use pattern piece (A) to cut a base from a stiff piece of cardboard. Cover with foil. Top with cookie base (A). Using small amounts of the canned frosting, attach the 4 cookie walls (B,C,D,E) to the cookie base (A) and to each other at the edges. Attach the cookie roof (F) to the walls with frosting. Let dry overnight.**

Decorating: **Use the frosting to attach decorations to the doghouse. Here are some suggestions:**
● **Trim the house corners with red licorice.**
● **Use pieces of red licorice to make a window and to spell out the dog's name.**
● **Use candy canes for the door and assorted candies for landscaping.**
● **Shingle nonpareils or pastel wafer candies on roof, starting at bottom and overlapping to top.**

Peanutty Brownies

¼ cup butter *or* margarine (½ stick) 2 squares (2 ounces) un-sweetened chocolate	● Turn oven to 350°. Grease a 9x9x2-inch baking pan with a little shortening. In a medium saucepan melt butter or margarine and chocolate over low heat, stirring often with a wooden spoon. Remove the saucepan from the heat and let cool about 15 minutes.
1 cup sugar ⅓ cup peanut butter	● Stir in sugar and peanut butter.
2 eggs ½ teaspoon vanilla	● Add eggs and vanilla and beat with wooden spoon till well mixed.
½ cup all-purpose flour ½ teaspoon baking powder ½ teaspoon salt	● In a small mixing bowl stir together flour, baking powder, and salt. Add to chocolate mixture in saucepan and beat with wooden spoon till smooth.
¼ cup chopped peanuts	● Stir in peanuts. Pour into the greased baking pan.
	● Bake in the 350° oven about 20 minutes or till edges are firm. Cool in pan on a cooling rack. Cut into bars. Makes 36 bars.

Chocolate and peanut butter go together like a hand in a cookie jar. These fudgy brownies are made with both peanut butter and peanuts.

If you don't have the 2 squares of unsweetened chocolate needed for this recipe, stir 6 tablespoons of unsweetened cocoa powder into the flour mixture and increase the butter or margarine you use to 6 tablespoons.

Hopscotch Squares

Also pictured on page 9—

Brown sugar and butter give these squares their butterscotch flavor.

¼ **cup butter *or* margarine (½ stick)**	● Turn oven to 350°. Grease an 8x8x2-inch baking pan with a little shortening. In a medium saucepan melt butter or margarine over low heat. Remove saucepan from heat.
1 **cup packed brown sugar**	● With a wooden spoon stir in the brown sugar.
1 **egg** ½ **teaspoon vanilla**	● Add egg and vanilla. Beat with wooden spoon till well mixed.
1 **cup all-purpose flour** 1 **teaspoon baking powder** ⅛ **teaspoon salt** ½ **cup chopped walnuts**	● In a medium mixing bowl stir together flour, baking powder, and salt. Add flour mixture and chopped walnuts to brown sugar mixture and stir till well mixed.
	● Spread batter in the greased baking pan. Bake in the 350° oven for 20 to 25 minutes or till edges are firm. Cut into squares while warm. Makes 25 squares.

Do you ever end up with crooked brownies? Here is a way to help you cut them straight.

Using a ruler, measure and mark the brownies into the size pieces you want. Then stick in toothpicks to show you where to cut. Lay the ruler across the top of the pan from toothpick to toothpick. Moving the knife along the ruler, cut across the pan of brownies.

Peanut Butter Wonder Bars

½ cup butter *or* margarine (1 stick) ½ cup peanut butter ½ cup packed brown sugar	● Turn oven to 350°. Grease a 15x10x1-inch baking pan with a little shortening. In a large mixer bowl beat butter or margarine and peanut butter with electric mixer on medium speed about 30 seconds. Add brown sugar and beat till fluffy.	**Wonder why they're so good and chewy? It's the combination of peanut butter, honey, raisins, and rolled oats.**
1 egg ½ cup honey 2 tablespoons milk	● Add egg, honey, and milk. Beat well.	**The directions say to make these bars in a 15x10x1-inch baking pan. If you don't have a pan that size, use two 9x9x2-inch baking pans instead and bake in the 350° oven about 18 minutes or till the bars test done.**
1½ cups all-purpose flour ½ teaspoon baking soda ½ teaspoon baking powder ½ teaspoon salt	● In a medium mixing bowl stir together flour, baking soda, baking powder, and salt. With electric mixer on low speed gradually add the flour mixture to the peanut butter mixture, beating till the ingredients are well mixed.	
1 cup quick-cooking rolled oats 1 cup raisins	● With a wooden spoon stir the quick-cooking rolled oats and the raisins into the mixture. Spread the batter evenly in the greased baking pan.	
	● Bake in the 350° oven for 20 to 25 minutes or till a toothpick inserted near center comes out clean. Cool in the baking pan on a cooling rack. Cut into bars. Makes 48 bars.	

Chocolate River Bars

½ cup butter *or* margarine (1 stick) ½ cup packed brown sugar ¼ cup sugar	● Turn oven to 350°. Grease a 13x9x2-inch baking pan. In a large mixer bowl beat butter or margarine with electric mixer on medium speed till softened (about 30 seconds). Add brown sugar and sugar and beat till fluffy.
1 egg ½ teaspoon vanilla *or* almond extract	● Add egg and extract. Beat well.
1¼ cups all-purpose flour ½ teaspoon baking soda ½ teaspoon salt	● In a medium mixing bowl stir together flour, baking soda, and salt. With mixer on low speed gradually add flour mixture to butter mixture, beating till well mixed.
1 6-ounce package (1 cup) semisweet chocolate pieces	● Spread batter in the greased baking pan. Sprinkle chocolate pieces evenly over top of batter.
	● Place in the 350° oven about 2 minutes or just till chocolate pieces soften. Remove pan from oven. With a table knife, swirl the melted chocolate pieces into the batter as shown below.
	● Return the pan to the 350° oven. Bake 12 to 15 minutes more or till golden. Cool in pan on a cooling rack. Cut into bars. Makes 32 bars.

Little chocolate rivers ripple through these simple bar cookies. The flavor will remind you of chocolate chip cookies.

With a knife, swirl the softened chocolate pieces back and forth through the batter to make "chocolate rivers." Then finish baking the bars till they're golden brown.

Applecadabra Bars

1 cup sugar ½ cup shortening	● Turn oven to 350°. Grease a 15x10x1-inch baking pan with a little shortening. In a large mixer bowl beat together sugar and the ½ cup shortening with electric mixer on medium speed till mixture is fluffy.
1 8½-ounce can (1 cup) applesauce 1 teaspoon vanilla	● Add applesauce and vanilla. Beat well.
2 cups all-purpose flour 1 teaspoon baking soda ½ teaspoon salt ¼ teaspoon ground nutmeg ⅛ teaspoon ground cloves	● In a medium mixing bowl stir together flour, baking soda, salt, nutmeg, and cloves. With mixer on low speed gradually add flour mixture to applesauce mixture, beating till well mixed.
1 cup raisins	● With a wooden spoon stir the raisins into the batter. Spread the batter evenly in the greased baking pan.
2 tablespoons butter *or* margarine ½ cup finely crushed bran flakes (about 1 cup uncrushed)	● In a small saucepan melt butter or margarine over low heat. Remove from heat. Stir in crushed bran flakes just till combined. Sprinkle over batter in baking pan. Pat gently.
	● Bake in the 350° oven about 15 minutes or till a toothpick inserted near center comes out clean. Let cool in the baking pan on a cooling rack. Cut into bars. Makes 40 bars.

Watch these crunch-topped bars disappear before your very eyes.

Here are two tricks for crushing bran flakes without making a mess. Either measure about 1 cup bran flakes into a plastic bag and crush them with your hand, or fill a 2-cup measuring cup about half-full with bran flakes and crush them with a spoon.

2-Carrot Diamonds

2 eggs 1 cup packed brown sugar ⅔ cup cooking oil	● Turn oven to 350°. Grease a 15x10x1-inch baking pan with a little shortening. In a large mixing bowl beat together eggs, brown sugar, and oil with a wooden spoon till well combined.
1¾ cups all-purpose flour 1 teaspoon baking powder 1 teaspoon ground cinnamon ¼ teaspoon salt	● In a medium mixing bowl stir together flour, baking powder, cinnamon, and salt. Gradually add to egg mixture, stirring with wooden spoon till well mixed.
1 cup shredded carrots (2 to 3 medium carrots) ¾ cup raisins	● Stir in shredded carrots and the raisins. Pour batter into the greased baking pan and spread evenly.
	● Bake in the 350° oven for 22 to 25 minutes or till a toothpick inserted near center comes out clean. Let cool in pan on a cooling rack.
	● When cool, spread with Cream Cheese Frosting. Cut into diamonds. Makes 42 bars.

Cream Cheese Frosting: In a medium mixing bowl beat together two 3-ounce packages *cream cheese*, ¼ cup *butter or margarine*, and 2 teaspoons *vanilla* with wooden spoon till light and fluffy. Gradually add 4 cups sifted *powdered sugar*, beating till smooth.

Diamonds are a kid's best friend when they taste this good. They'll remind you of moist carrot cake.

Cut the diamonds as shown in this drawing to get the most bars possible. First cut 6 equal rows (5 lines) even with the long sides of the pan. Then, cut slanting lines across the pan (at a 45-degree angle), keeping the lines as even as you can.

Chocolate Brownie Dominoes

¼ cup butter *or* margarine (½ stick) ½ cup sugar	● Turn oven to 350°. Grease an 8x8x2-inch baking pan with a little shortening. In a small mixer bowl beat butter or margarine with electric mixer on medium speed till softened (about 30 seconds). Add sugar and beat till fluffy.	**Turn chocolate brownies into delicious dominoes with some white frosting and tiny chocolate chips.**
2 eggs	● Add eggs. Beat well.	
¾ cup chocolate-flavored syrup ⅔ cup all-purpose flour	● Add chocolate-flavored syrup and flour. Beat till well mixed. Spread the batter in the greased baking pan.	
	● Bake in the 350° oven for 30 to 35 minutes or till a toothpick inserted near center comes out clean. Let cool in pan on cooling rack.	
Butter Frosting *or* canned vanilla frosting Miniature semisweet chocolate pieces	● When cool, spread with Butter Frosting or canned vanilla frosting. Cut into 24 rectangular bars. Follow directions at right for using chocolate pieces to make bars look like dominoes. Makes 24 bars.	**Draw a line across each frosted bar with a toothpick to make 2 squares. Then give the dominoes dots by putting up to 6 tiny chocolate chips, point down, in each square.**

Butter Frosting: In a small mixer bowl beat 2 tablespoons *butter or margarine* with electric mixer on medium speed till softened. Gradually add ⅔ cup sifted *powdered sugar,* beating well. Beat in 2 teaspoons *milk* and ½ teaspoon *vanilla.* Gradually beat in ⅔ cup more sifted *powdered sugar.* Beat in additional *milk* (about 1 teaspoon), if necessary, to make a frosting that is easy to spread.

Monkey Bars

¾ cup butter *or* margarine (1½ sticks) ⅔ cup sugar ⅔ cup packed brown sugar	● Turn oven to 350°. Grease a 15x10x1-inch baking pan with a little shortening. In a large mixer bowl beat butter or margarine with electric mixer on medium speed till softened (about 30 seconds). Add sugar and brown sugar and beat till fluffy.
1 egg 1 teaspoon vanilla	● Add egg and vanilla. Beat well.
1 cup mashed ripe bananas (3 medium)	● Stir in mashed bananas.
2¼ cups all-purpose flour 2 teaspoons baking powder ½ teaspoon salt	● In a medium mixing bowl stir together flour, baking powder, and salt. With mixer on low speed gradually add the flour mixture to the banana mixture, beating till well mixed.
1 6-ounce package (1 cup) semisweet chocolate pieces	● With a wooden spoon stir in semisweet chocolate pieces. Spread batter in the greased baking pan.
Powdered sugar (optional)	● Bake in the 350° oven about 25 minutes or till a toothpick inserted near center comes out clean. Let cool in the pan on a cooling rack. Sprinkle with powdered sugar if desired. Cut into bars. Makes 48 bars.

The flavors of chocolate and bananas in a cakey bar cookie.

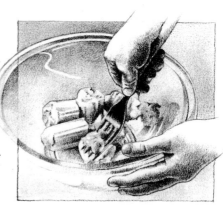

Mashing bananas is a step even the most inexperienced little cooks can do. Peel a banana and place it in a bowl. Cut it into 3 or 4 pieces with the side of a fork. Then use the prongs of the fork to mash the pieces against the side of the bowl. Spoon the mashed banana into a measuring cup. Do the same with the rest of the bananas till you get 1 level cup of mashed bananas.

Walkie-Toffee Bars

1 cup butter *or* margarine (2 sticks) 1 cup packed brown sugar	● Turn oven to 350°. In a large mixer bowl beat butter or margarine with electric mixer on medium speed till softened (about 30 seconds). Add brown sugar and beat till fluffy.
1 egg 2 teaspoons vanilla	● Add egg and vanilla. Beat well.
2 cups all-purpose flour	● With mixer on low speed gradually add flour to butter mixture, beating till well mixed. Spread batter evenly in an ungreased 15x10x1-inch baking pan.
1 6-ounce package (1 cup) semisweet chocolate pieces	● Bake in the 350° oven for 20 to 25 minutes or till top is golden brown and a toothpick inserted near center comes out clean. Immediately sprinkle chocolate pieces over top and let stand about 2 minutes or just till chocolate pieces soften. Spread chocolate evenly.
½ cup chopped walnuts *or* pecans	● Sprinkle with the chopped nuts. Let cool in pan on a cooling rack. Chill in the refrigerator about 30 minutes or till chocolate is firm. Cut into bars. Store in a covered container. Makes 48 bars.

Do you want to send the message that you like someone? Send it loud and clear by making *Walkie-Toffee Bars.*

Toffee is a hard candy made with brown sugar and butter. You'll often see it spread with chocolate and sprinkled with nuts. These cookies are called toffee bars because they have those same wonderful flavors.

You'll know the bars are done when you stick a toothpick near the center of the uncut bars and it's clean when you pull it out.

Hidden-Treasure Ginger Bars

½ cup butter *or* margarine (1 stick) ½ cup packed brown sugar	● Turn oven to 350°. Grease a 13x9x2-inch baking pan with a little shortening. Coat lightly with flour. In a large mixer bowl beat butter or margarine with electric mixer on medium speed till softened (about 30 seconds). Add brown sugar and beat till fluffy.	These soft bars look and taste like gingerbread. But take a bite and you'll find little gumdrop treasures buried in each bar.
½ cup light molasses 1 egg	● Add molasses and egg. Beat well.	Long ago, people thought ginger cured stomach aches. Today we use ginger to flavor foods that cure, not stomach aches, but growling stomachs.
1¼ cups all-purpose flour 1 teaspoon baking powder ¾ teaspoon ground ginger ¾ teaspoon ground cinnamon ½ teaspoon salt ¼ teaspoon baking soda	● In a medium mixing bowl stir together flour, baking powder, ginger, cinnamon, salt, and baking soda. Gradually add *half* of the flour mixture to the molasses mixture, beating well.	
⅓ cup water	● Beat in the water and then the remaining flour mixture till well mixed.	
¾ cup snipped gumdrops	● With a wooden spoon stir in gumdrops. Pour batter into the greased and floured baking pan. Spread the batter evenly in the pan.	
Powdered sugar (optional)	● Bake in the 350° oven for 20 to 25 minutes or till a toothpick inserted near center comes out clean. Cool in the baking pan on a cooling rack. Sprinkle with powdered sugar if desired. Cut into bars. Makes 36 bars.	

Use kitchen scissors to snip the gumdrops. Cut small gumdrops in half and cut large ones into 4 or more pieces.

Slice-'Em-Up Cookies

| ½ cup butter *or* margarine (1 stick)
¾ cup sugar | ● In a large mixer bowl beat butter or margarine with electric mixer on medium speed till softened (about 30 seconds). Add sugar and beat till fluffy. |

This homemade version of slice-and-bake cookies will keep in your freezer up to 6 months. When you want fresh cookies, unwrap a roll, slice off as many cookies as you need, and bake.

| 1 egg
2 teaspoons vanilla | ● Add egg and vanilla. Beat well. |

| 1¾ cups all-purpose flour
½ teaspoon baking powder
¼ teaspoon salt | ● In a medium mixing bowl stir together flour, baking powder, and salt. With mixer on low speed gradually add flour mixture to butter mixture, beating till well mixed. Stir in the last portion of the flour mixture with a wooden spoon or mix it in with your hands. |

| ½ cup finely chopped nuts, chocolate-flavored sprinkles, colored sugar, *or* grated coconut (optional) | ● If dough seems too soft to shape, chill in the freezer about 20 minutes. Divide dough in half. Shape each half into a roll 6 inches long. Roll in chopped nuts, chocolate-flavored sprinkles, colored sugar, or coconut if desired. Wrap rolls in clear plastic wrap. Freeze at least 4 hours or up to 6 months. |

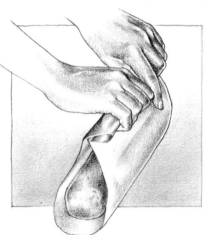

● When you want to bake the cookies, turn oven to 375°. Grease cookie sheets with a little shortening. Unwrap rolls. With a sharp knife, slice the frozen rolls crosswise so the slices are ⅛ inch thick. Place slices about 1 inch apart on the greased cookie sheets.

Wrap the dough tightly in clear plastic wrap before freezing. Be sure to leave enough wrap at the ends so you can tuck the wrap snugly under the roll.

● Bake in the 375° oven about 10 minutes or till edges of cookies are light brown. With a pancake turner lift the cookies onto a cooling rack to cool. Makes about 48 cookies.

Chocolate Slice-'Em-Up Cookies: Prepare Slice-'Em-Up Cookies as above, *except* add ¼ cup *unsweetened cocoa powder* with the sugar.

Peanut Butter and Jelly Posies

½ cup butter *or* margarine (1 stick)
½ cup peanut butter
⅓ cup sugar
⅓ cup packed brown sugar

● In a large mixer bowl beat butter or margarine and peanut butter with electric mixer on medium speed about 30 seconds. Add sugar and brown sugar and beat till fluffy.

Here are the flavors of kids' favorite sandwich in a cookie that looks like a flower! Make the peanut butter cookie dough, shape, and freeze. When you want fresh cookies, fill with jelly and bake (or bake, then fill later).

3 tablespoons orange juice

● Add orange juice. Beat well.

1½ cups all-purpose flour
1½ teaspoons baking soda
¼ teaspoon salt

● In a medium mixing bowl stir together flour, baking soda, and salt. With mixer on low speed gradually add flour mixture to the peanut butter mixture, beating till well mixed.

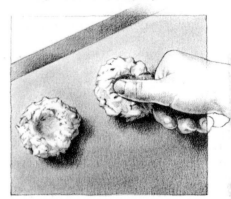

● With your hands, shape the dough into 1-inch balls. Place about 1 inch apart on an ungreased cookie sheet. Press down the center of each ball with your thumb.

To make the centers for the flowers, press down the middle of the balls of dough with your thumb.

● Place cookie sheet in freezer and freeze till dough is firm. Remove frozen pieces of dough from cookie sheet and place in freezer bags. Seal, label, and freeze for up to 6 months.

● When you want to bake the cookies, turn oven to 350°. Place frozen pieces of dough about 1 inch apart on ungreased cookie sheet.

Your favorite jam *or* jelly

● Fill centers with about ¼ teaspoon jam or jelly (or leave unfilled). Bake in the 350° oven for 10 to 12 minutes or till golden. Let cool on cookie sheet 2 minutes. With a pancake turner lift cookies onto a cooling rack to finish cooling. (If cookies were baked unfilled, fill the centers with jam or jelly just before serving.) Makes about 36 cookies.

If you fill the centers of the cookies before baking, the jam or jelly will bake into the cookies and you can stack them for storing. If you fill the centers just before serving, store in a single layer any cookies that aren't eaten so the jelly in one cookie won't stick to another cookie.

Kangaroo Sugar Pockets

Pictured on page 9—

½ cup butter *or* margarine (1 stick) ½ cup shortening 1 cup sugar	● In a large mixer bowl beat butter or margarine and shortening with electric mixer on medium speed about 30 seconds. Add the 1 cup sugar and beat till the mixture is fluffy.
1 egg 2 tablespoons milk ½ teaspoon vanilla	● Add egg, milk, and vanilla. Beat well.
2¼ cups all-purpose flour ½ teaspoon baking soda ½ teaspoon salt	● In a medium mixing bowl stir together flour, baking soda, and salt. With mixer on low speed gradually add the flour mixture to the butter mixture, beating till well mixed.
	● Cover and chill dough in the freezer about 20 minutes or till firm enough to handle. Divide dough in half. With your hands, shape each half of the dough into a roll 3 inches thick and about 3 inches long. Wrap in clear plastic wrap. Freeze at least 6 hours or up to 6 months.
	● When you want to bake the cookies, turn oven to 375°. Unwrap one roll of dough. With a sharp knife, slice the roll crosswise to make 16 slices that are about ⅛ inch thick.
Apple, blueberry, cherry, *or* peach pie filling, your favorite jam *or* jelly, peanut butter, chopped nuts, semisweet chocolate pieces, raisins, *or* toasted coconut Sugar	● Place *half* of the slices about 2 inches apart on an ungreased cookie sheet. In the center of the circles, place 2 teaspoons of desired filling (or a combination of fillings). Top each with a plain circle of dough. Press a floured fork around the edges to seal well. Sprinkle with a little sugar.
	● Bake in the 375° oven for 12 to 15 minutes or till edges of cookies are light brown. With a pancake turner lift cookies onto a cooling rack to cool. Repeat with the remaining roll of dough when desired. Makes about 16 large cookies.

"Look, they're puffing up and getting big!" squealed our young cookie testers, watching through the oven window. These two-fisted sugar cookies were a hit with the kids. They especially liked biting into the pockets of sweet surprises.

Fill some pockets with pie filling, others with jam or jelly, some with peanut butter, and still others with nuts, chocolate, raisins, or coconut. Or combine some of the fillings, using a total of 2 teaspoons in each pocket.

On-the-Spot Cookies

½ cup butter *or* margarine (1 stick)	● In a large mixer bowl beat butter or margarine with electric mixer on medium speed till softened (about 30 seconds).
½ cup sugar ½ cup packed brown sugar	● Add sugar and brown sugar and beat till fluffy.
1 egg ½ teaspoon vanilla	● Add egg and vanilla. Beat well.
¾ cup all-purpose flour ½ teaspoon baking soda ¼ teaspoon salt	● In a small mixing bowl stir together flour, baking soda, and salt. With mixer on low speed gradually add flour mixture to butter mixture, beating till well mixed.
1½ cups quick-cooking rolled oats ½ cup candy-coated milk chocolate pieces	● Stir in oats and candy-coated milk chocolate pieces.
	● With your hands, shape into 1-inch balls. Place on ungreased cookie sheet. Place cookie sheet in freezer.
	● When cookie dough is frozen, remove the balls of dough from the cookie sheet. Place dough in freezer bags. Seal, label, and freeze up to 6 months.
	● When you want to bake the cookies, turn oven to 375°. Remove balls of dough from freezer bag. Place about 2 inches apart on ungreased cookie sheets.
	● Bake in the 375° oven for 10 to 12 minutes or till golden. With a pancake turner lift cookies onto a cooling rack to cool. Makes about 42 cookies.

Crispy oatmeal cookies made with colorful chocolate candies. Keep the dough for these "spotted" cookies in your freezer so you can bake them "on the spot."

If you like, you can freeze the dough in one piece in a freezer container. When you're ready to bake, let the dough stand at room temperature about 15 minutes to soften. Shape into 1-inch balls and follow the baking directions in the recipe.

Lollipop Cookies

Cookies on a stick that start with a cookie mix. Decorate each lollipop before baking.

1 package 3-dozen-size sugar, oatmeal, *or* peanut butter cookie mix	● Turn oven to 375°. Grease cookie sheets if necessary (check cookie mix package). Prepare cookie dough according to directions on package.
12 to 14 wooden sticks	● Roll dough with your hands into 1½-inch balls. Put about 2 inches apart on cookie sheets. Insert a wooden stick halfway into each ball of dough.
Sugar	● Dip a flat-bottomed glass in some sugar, then use to flatten cookies.
Assorted decorations (red cinnamon candies; hard candy; sliced gumdrops; raisins; snipped dried fruit; *or* chocolate, butterscotch, *or* peanut butter-flavored pieces)	● Decorate cookies as desired with candies, fruits, or chocolate, butterscotch, or peanut butter-flavored pieces.
	● Bake in the 375° oven according to times on cookie mix package. With pancake turner lift cookies onto cooling rack to cool. Makes 12 to 14 cookies.

Roll dough into balls about the size of walnuts.

Push wooden sticks halfway into sides of balls.

Flatten cookies with a sugared, flat-bottomed glass. Decorate and bake.

Spice Cake Cookies

Pictured on page 69—

1 package 1-layer-size spice cake mix ⅓ cup shortening 1 egg	● Turn oven to 375°. In a small mixer bowl stir together dry cake mix, shortening, and egg. Beat with electric mixer on medium speed till well mixed.
½ cup chopped nuts (optional)	● With a wooden spoon stir in chopped nuts if desired.
	● With your hands, shape dough into 1-inch balls or drop by rounded teaspoons about 2 inches apart onto ungreased cookie sheets.
	● Bake in the 375° oven for 10 to 12 minutes or till centers are slightly puffed and edges are firm. Let cookies cool on the cookie sheets 1 minute. With a pancake turner lift cookies onto a cooling rack to finish cooling.
Canned creamy white frosting	● When cool, frost cookies with creamy white frosting. Makes about 30 cookies.

Chocolate Cake Cookies: Prepare Spice Cake Cookies as above, *except* substitute 1 package *1-layer-size devil's food cake mix* for the spice cake mix. Frost with canned *chocolate frosting*.

For easy, delicious cookies, these take the cake! That's because they're made with a cake mix. They taste like spice cake and have a creamy white frosting. It's like having a lot of little cakes to eat instead of one big one.

If you keep these crispy cookies overnight in a tightly covered container, they'll soften up and seem even more like cake.

Top freshly baked cookies with pudding and fruit to make a great cookie dessert for the whole family.

Fresh-Fruit Cookie Tarts

1 roll refrigerated oatmeal-raisin, peanut butter, *or* sugar cookie dough	● Turn oven to 375°. Unwrap roll of cookie dough. With a sharp knife, cut roll into 9 equal slices. Place 4 inches apart on ungreased cookie sheets. Flatten slightly with your hand.
	● Bake in the 375° oven for 9 to 11 minutes or till cookies are light golden brown. With a pancake turner lift the cookies onto a cooling rack to cool.
Desired fruit, such as strawberries, bananas, seedless grapes, oranges, kiwi, *or* apples	● Just before serving, cut up desired fruits. For strawberries, cut out stems and slice. For bananas, peel and slice. For grapes, cut in half. For oranges, cut off outer peel and white part of peel. Section oranges. For kiwi, slice off ends, peel fruit, and slice. For apples, cut in half, then in quarters. Remove stem and seeds. Slice apple.
1 16-ounce can vanilla *or* tapioca pudding Raisins *or* toasted coconut (optional)	● Spoon some vanilla or tapioca pudding over each cookie, spreading it to the edges with the back of the spoon. (If any pudding is left over, cover and refrigerate for another dessert.) Decorate cookies with cut-up fruit. If desired, add raisins or toasted coconut. Serve immediately. Makes 9 cookies.

Use cut-up fruit to make designs or faces on the pudding-topped cookies. Wedges of an orange or peach become butterfly wings or happy smiles. A strawberry cut in half can be flower petals or a lady's mouth. Grape halves make eyes, noses, or beaded necklaces. Nuts are good noses, and toasted coconut looks like frizzy hair. See what other foods you have around that would look and taste good on your cookie tarts.

Craters of Coconut

1 roll refrigerated sugar cookie dough	● Turn oven to 350°. Grease 1¾-inch-diameter muffin pans with a little shortening. Unwrap roll of sugar cookie dough. With a sharp knife, cut roll of dough into 9 equal slices. Cut each slice into 4 equal pieces. Put one piece in each muffin cup.	**In the oven a gooey filling made of coconut and crushed toffee bars bubbles up inside these cookie craters.**
	● Bake in the 350° oven for 8 minutes.	
3 tablespoons brown sugar **1 tablespoon butter *or* margarine, softened** **1 tablespoon milk** **½ cup flaked coconut** **½ cup crushed chocolate-coated English toffee bars**	● Meanwhile, in a small mixing bowl stir together brown sugar and softened butter or margarine. Add milk and stir till well mixed. Stir in flaked coconut and crushed toffee bars.	**Making craters is as easy as 1, 2, 3, 4:** **1 Grease the little muffin cups with shortening.** **2 Put one piece of cookie dough in each muffin cup. (You don't need to press it into the pan because it will spread and puff up in the oven.)**
	● Remove muffin pans from oven. Put a rounded teaspoon of the coconut-toffee bar mixture in the center of each partially baked cookie.	**3 Bake for 8 minutes.**
	● Return the muffin pans to the 350° oven. Bake 2 to 3 minutes more or till cookies are golden. Cool in muffin pans on a cooling rack at least 10 minutes. Carefully remove cookies from muffin pans. Makes 36 cookies.	**4 Fill the craters with the coconut mixture. Bake them 2 to 3 minutes more. Let them cool about 10 minutes in the pan before taking them out.**

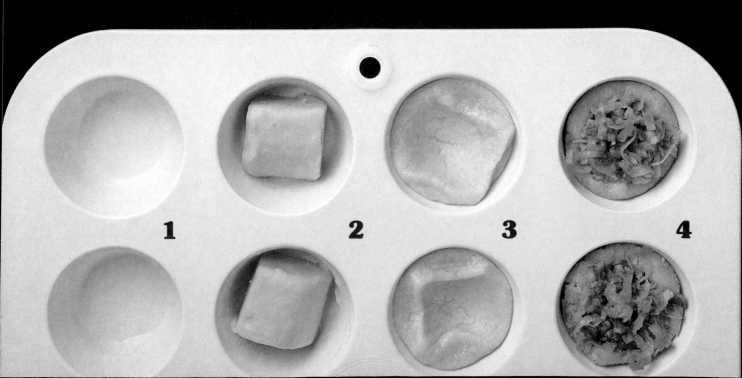

1   2   3   4

Easy-as-Pie Cookies

1 package piecrust mix (for 2-crust pie) ¾ cup presweetened cocoa powder ⅓ cup sugar ½ teaspoon ground cinnamon ¼ teaspoon baking soda	● Turn oven to 350°. In a large mixer bowl crumble the piecrust mix with your fingers. Stir in the presweetened cocoa powder, sugar, ground cinnamon, and baking soda.
1 egg ⅓ cup milk 1 teaspoon vanilla	● Add the egg, milk, and vanilla. Beat with an electric mixer on medium speed till well mixed.
½ cup chopped nuts (optional)	● Stir in chopped nuts if desired. Drop dough by rounded teaspoons about 2 inches apart onto ungreased cookie sheets.
	● Bake in the 350° oven 10 to 12 minutes or till edges are firm. With pancake turner lift cookies onto cooling rack.
Canned chocolate frosting	● When cool, frost cookies with chocolate frosting. Makes about 32 cookies.

They look like chocolate cookies, taste like brownies, and are made with a piecrust mix!

About 400 years ago, the Spanish put cinnamon in their hot chocolate and found out how good it tasted. People have mixed chocolate and cinnamon in foods ever since. See whether you can taste the cinnamon in these cocoa-flavored cookies.

Blueberry Snack Bars
(see recipe, page 70)

Easy-as-Pie Cookies

Lemon Lickety-Splits

The texture of these cake-like cookies comes from biscuit mix, and their great flavor from instant pudding mix. We call them lickety-splits because they're quick to make and even quicker to disappear.

1 egg ¼ cup milk	● Turn oven to 350°. Grease cookie sheets with a little shortening. In a medium mixing bowl beat together egg and milk with a fork.
1 cup packaged biscuit mix 1 package 4-serving-size *instant* lemon pudding mix	● With a wooden spoon stir in dry biscuit mix and dry pudding mix just till well mixed.
½ cup raisins *or* semi-sweet chocolate pieces	● Stir in raisins or chocolate pieces. Drop dough by rounded teaspoons about 2 inches apart onto the greased cookie sheets.
	● Bake in the 350° oven for 10 to 12 minutes or till light brown on top. With a pancake turner lift cookies onto a cooling rack. Makes about 20 cookies.

Banana Lickety-Splits: Prepare Lemon Lickety-Splits as above, *except* substitute 1 package 4-serving-size *instant banana cream pudding mix* for the lemon pudding mix.

Lemon Lickety-Splits

Spice Cake Cookies
(see recipe, page 65)

Chocolate Puddle Peanut Butter Cookies

2 sticks piecrust mix, crumbled
1 3-ounce can (2 cups) chow mein noodles, crushed to measure 1 cup
½ cup packed brown sugar

● Turn oven to 375°. In a large mixing bowl stir together the crumbled piecrust mix, the crushed chow mein noodles, and the brown sugar.

Each crunchy peanut butter cookie is topped with a chocolate-covered peanut butter cup. The candies melt into neat little puddles in the tops of the cookies as they bake.

1 egg
⅓ cup peanut butter
½ teaspoon vanilla

● Stir in egg, peanut butter, and vanilla. Mix with your hands till well combined. Shape into 36 balls. Place 2 inches apart on ungreased cookie sheets. With your thumb or the back of a spoon, make a large well in the center of each ball.

1 9-ounce package (36 candies) bite-size chocolate-covered peanut butter cups

● Bake in the 375° oven for 8 minutes. Press a candy in each center. Return cookie sheet to 375° oven. Bake 2 to 3 minutes more or till candies are melted. With a pancake turner lift cookies onto cooling rack. Makes 36 cookies.

Blueberry Snack Bars

Pictured on page 68–

1 13-ounce package blueberry muffin mix
½ cup granola
½ cup flaked coconut
¼ teaspoon ground cinnamon

● Turn oven to 350°. Grease a 13x9x2-inch baking pan with a little shortening. In a large mixing bowl stir together dry muffin mix, granola, coconut, and cinnamon. Drain blueberries from muffin mix package.

Put together a blueberry muffin mix, granola, coconut, an egg, and orange juice, and what do you have? No, not breakfast, but moist bars that you can eat as a snack, for dessert, or even as part of your breakfast.

1 egg
¾ cup orange juice

● In a small mixing bowl beat together the egg and orange juice with a fork. With a wooden spoon gently stir in the drained blueberries.

● With a wooden spoon stir egg mixture into granola mixture just till all of the dry ingredients are moistened. Spoon the batter into the greased baking pan and spread evenly.

Because these bars are so moist, it's easiest to cut them with a serrated knife. That's the kind of knife with teeth on the cutting edge. Cut the bars with a gentle sawing motion rather than with one long stroke.

Powdered sugar

● Bake in the 350° oven about 20 minutes or till top is light brown. Cool in the baking pan on a cooling rack. Sprinkle with powdered sugar. Cut into bars. Makes 24 bars.

Burger Bites

Few drops water 1 **drop green food coloring** ¼ **cup flaked coconut**	● In a small screw-top jar combine the few drops water and the green food coloring. Add coconut; cover and shake till all of the coconut is tinted. Set aside.
48 **vanilla wafers** 24 **chocolate-covered pepper-mint patties**	● Turn oven to 350°. Follow directions below for assembling cookies using vanilla wafers and peppermint patties.
Water **Sesame seed** *or* **poppy seed**	● Brush tops with water and sprinkle with sesame seed or poppy seed. Makes 24 cookies.

Tiny hamburger-shaped cookies with vanilla wafer "sesame seed buns," peppermint "meat" patties, and coconut "lettuce."

1 Place half of the vanilla wafers, flat side up, on an ungreased cookie sheet. Top each with a chocolate-covered peppermint patty. Place in the 350° oven about 1 minute or just till chocolate begins to soften.

2 Sprinkle each with ½ teaspoon tinted coconut. Top with another vanilla wafer. Press gently.

3 With a clean paint brush, pastry brush, or your finger, brush the top vanilla wafers with just enough water to moisten so the sesame seed or poppy seed will stick.

4 Sprinkle each cookie with a little sesame seed or poppy seed and serve.

Apricot Bowling Balls

¾ **cup Grape Nuts cereal** ¾ **cup finely crushed graham crackers** ¾ **cup finely snipped dried apricots** ½ **cup finely chopped pecans** ½ **cup sifted powdered sugar**	● In a medium mixing bowl stir together the Grape Nuts cereal, finely crushed graham crackers, finely snipped dried apricots, finely chopped pecans, and the ½ cup sifted powdered sugar.
¼ **cup light corn syrup** 1 **tablespoon orange juice *or* water**	● Stir in corn syrup and orange juice or water. With buttered hands, shape into ¾-inch balls.
¼ **cup toasted wheat germ *or* sifted powdered sugar**	● Roll the balls in wheat germ or powdered sugar. Store in a covered container. Makes about 36 cookies.

If you like cookies, but don't like to bake, these bowling balls will be right up your alley. Just mix and shape into balls.

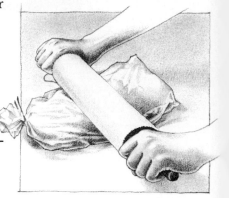

To finely crush the graham crackers, put about 5 squares at a time in a plastic bag. Close the bag and crush the crackers with a rolling pin.

Fudged Cookies

2 **cups sugar** ¼ **cup unsweetened cocoa powder**	● In a heavy large saucepan stir together sugar and cocoa powder.
½ **cup milk**	● Stir in milk.
½ **cup butter *or* margarine (1 stick)** 1 **tablespoon light corn syrup**	● Add butter or margarine and corn syrup. Bring to boiling, stirring once in a while. Boil hard for 3 minutes.
¼ **cup peanut butter** 2 **cups quick-cooking rolled oats**	● Stir in peanut butter, then oats. Return mixture to boiling. Remove from heat.
	● Beat with a wooden spoon about 5 minutes or till slightly thickened. Immediately drop by rounded teaspoons onto waxed paper. (If mixture spreads too much, beat a little longer.) Let cool till firm. Makes about 36 cookies.

These are called *Fudged Cookies* for two reasons: you fudge in making them because you don't bake them, and they taste so much like fudge you'll forget they're cookies.

This recipe is a good one to try with an adult. You need strong arms to handle the saucepan and to stir the fudgy batter.

Peanut Butter Meteors

Pictured on page 8–

½ cup packed brown sugar ½ cup peanut butter ¼ cup evaporated milk	● In a medium saucepan stir together brown sugar, peanut butter, and evaporated milk. Bring to boiling, stirring constantly, till brown sugar is dissolved and peanut butter is melted.
2½ cups crisp rice cereal *or* granola	● Remove from heat. Stir in crisp rice cereal or granola.
	● Drop by rounded teaspoons onto waxed paper. Cool till firm. Makes 36.

Use chunk-style peanut butter in these cereal cookies if you like to bite into little chunks of peanuts.

Popcorn Nibblers

¼ cup sugar ¼ cup light corn syrup	● In a medium saucepan stir together sugar and corn syrup. Cook and stir over medium heat till sugar is dissolved.
½ cup peanut butter	● Stir in peanut butter till smooth.
2 cups popped popcorn ½ cup chopped peanuts	● Stir in popcorn and chopped peanuts till thoroughly coated.
	● Drop by rounded teaspoons onto waxed paper. Cool till firm. Makes 24.

Popcorn and peanuts are great nibble foods. Smother them with a peanut butter coating to make chewy, candy-like cookies.

Making Popcorn

If you've never made popcorn by yourself before, ask an adult to help you. Here's what you do:
● Pour 1 tablespoon of *cooking oil* into a heavy 2-quart saucepan. Add 2 or 3 kernels of *unpopped popcorn.*
● Put the pan on the burner and turn to medium-high heat. Put on the lid and cook till you hear the corn pop.
● Take off the lid and add 3 tablespoons *unpopped popcorn.* Put on the lid and cook, shaking pan gently.
● When the popping slows down, turn off the burner. Keep shaking the pan till the corn stops popping.
● Empty popcorn into a bowl. Measure the amount you need for *Popcorn Nibblers* (2 cups), being careful not to use any unpopped kernels. Makes about 4 cups.

S'mple S'mores

½ cup butter *or* margarine (1 stick)	● Line a 9x9x2-inch baking pan with foil. Butter the foil. In a medium saucepan melt the ½ cup butter or margarine over medium-low heat.
½ cup sugar	● Remove from heat. Stir in the sugar.
2 eggs	● In a small bowl beat the eggs with a fork. Stir into butter mixture. Return to medium-low heat. Cook till bubbly, stirring constantly. Remove from heat.
1 teaspoon vanilla	● Stir in vanilla. Cool about 20 minutes.
5½ cups honey graham cereal	● Finely crush the cereal till it measures 1¾ cups. Stir the crushed cereal into the butter and egg mixture in the saucepan.
1½ cups tiny marshmallows	● Stir in marshmallows. Evenly spread the cereal mixture in the prepared pan.
½ cup milk chocolate pieces	● In a small saucepan melt the milk chocolate pieces over low heat, stirring constantly. Drizzle over the cereal mixture in the baking pan.
	● Cover and chill in the refrigerator for 1 to 2 hours or till the mixture is firm. Cut into bars. Store in the refrigerator. Makes 24 bars.

To make s'mores the regular way, you would roast marshmallows over a campfire and sandwich them with chocolate bars between graham crackers. These simple bars give you the flavors of s'mores when you don't have a campfire. Just mix in a saucepan, chill in a square pan, and cut into bars.

To melt chocolate, use *low* heat and stir *constantly* to keep the chocolate from scorching.

Crispy Crunch Bars

3 cups tiny marshmallows 3 tablespoons butter *or* margarine	● Line a 13x9x2-inch baking pan with foil. Butter the foil. In a large saucepan melt marshmallows and 3 tablespoons butter or margarine over low heat, stirring constantly till marshmallows are melted. Remove from heat.	Those popular bars that are chewy and crunchy at the same time. For a switch, use round toasted oat cereal or stir in raisins, peanuts, sunflower nuts, or gumdrops.
½ teaspoon vanilla 5 cups crisp rice cereal *or* round toasted oat cereal	● Stir in vanilla. Stir in *half* of the cereal at a time.	
1 cup raisins, peanuts, sunflower nuts, *or* snipped gumdrops (optional)	● Fold in raisins, peanuts, sunflower nuts, or snipped gumdrops if desired. Turn mixture into prepared pan. Press evenly with the back of a wooden spoon or with buttered hands. Cool. Cut into bars. Makes 24 bars.	

To get bars out of the pan easily, line the pan with foil, overlapping the sides. When the mixture cools, lift out with the foil "handles," then cut into bars.

No-Bake Snakes

¼ cup butter *or* margarine (½ stick) ¼ cup peanut butter	● In a medium saucepan melt the butter or margarine and peanut butter over low heat, stirring with a wooden spoon.	**You'll like these friendly creatures—they taste good, they're nutritious, and they're fun to make.**
½ cup honey 1 teaspoon vanilla	● Remove saucepan from heat. Stir in honey and vanilla.	
1½ cups quick-cooking rolled oats ½ cup toasted wheat germ ⅓ cup nonfat dry milk powder 2 tablespoons unsweetened cocoa powder ⅛ teaspoon ground cinnamon	● Stir in quick-cooking rolled oats, toasted wheat germ, nonfat dry milk powder, unsweetened cocoa powder, and ground cinnamon till well mixed.	
	● With your hands, shape the mixture into ropes about ½ inch thick and as long as you want.	
Sesame seed, toasted wheat germ, shredded coconut, *or* finely chopped nuts	● Place sesame seed, wheat germ, shredded coconut, or finely chopped nuts on a piece of waxed paper and roll snakes in it till coated.	**Make some snakes short, some snakes long; roll some in wheat germ or coconut, some in seed or nuts. When you're finished making them, put them in cages of upside-down plastic containers that fruits or vegetables come in at your grocery store.**
	● Place on waxed-paper-lined baking sheet. Chill in the refrigerator about 2 hours or till firm. Store in a covered container. Makes 72 inches of snakes.	

Pretzel Pile-Ups

2 cups coarsely crushed pretzels **¼ cup peanuts**	● In a large mixing bowl combine crushed pretzels and peanuts. Set aside.
½ of a 14-ounce can (about ⅔ cup) Eagle Brand sweetened condensed milk **½ cup semisweet chocolate pieces** **½ cup butterscotch pieces**	● In a medium saucepan combine sweetened condensed milk, chocolate pieces, and butterscotch pieces. Cook over low heat, stirring constantly, about 5 minutes or till pieces are melted. Remove the saucepan from heat.
¼ teaspoon vanilla	● Stir in vanilla.
	● Pour chocolate mixture over pretzel mixture in the bowl. Stir with a wooden spoon till thoroughly coated.
	● Drop by rounded teaspoons onto a waxed-paper-lined baking sheet. Cool (or chill in the refrigerator) till firm.
	● Store, covered, in the refrigerator. Makes about 36 cookies.

If you like chocolate-covered pretzels and chocolate-covered peanuts, you'll love these funny-looking snacks.

They're no trouble to make if you remember these easy "up" steps:
1. Crush up the pretzels.
2. Stir up the pretzels and peanuts.
3. Heat up the chocolate mixture.
4. Mix up the whole thing.
5. Spoon up the dough.
6. Eat up the cookies.

Bran New Chews

½ cup packed brown sugar **⅓ cup light corn syrup**	● In a medium saucepan stir together brown sugar and corn syrup with a wooden spoon. Bring to boiling, stirring constantly. Remove from heat.
¾ cup chunk-style peanut butter	● Stir in peanut butter till smooth.
2½ cups raisin bran cereal	● Stir in raisin bran cereal till well coated. Drop by rounded teaspoons onto waxed paper. Cool till cookies are firm. Store in a covered container. Makes about 36 cookies.

Here's how our young cookie tasters described these cookies:
"I see corn flakes." (Actually, it was raisin bran they saw.)
"Tastes like peanut butter."
"Chewy."
"Good!"

Whole Wheat Gingerbread People

These gingerbread cookies are especially for kids. The not-too-sticky dough is easy to roll out and the not-too-spicy cookies are crisp and wholesome. Pipe icing onto your cookies with a pastry tube and tip, or try *this* tip. Half-fill a heavy plastic sandwich bag with icing. With scissors, snip the very tip off one corner. Roll down the empty part of the bag and squeeze the icing out of the small hole.

1 cup butter *or* margarine (2 sticks) 1 cup packed brown sugar	● In a large mixer bowl beat butter or margarine with electric mixer on medium speed till softened (about 30 seconds). Add brown sugar and beat till fluffy.
1 egg ⅓ cup light molasses 1 tablespoon finely shredded orange peel 2 tablespoons orange juice	● Add the egg, light molasses, finely shredded orange peel, and orange juice. Beat the mixture well.
3 cups all-purpose flour 1 cup whole wheat flour 2 teaspoons ground cinnamon 1 teaspoon ground ginger ½ teaspoon baking soda ½ teaspoon salt ½ teaspoon ground cloves	● In a large mixing bowl stir together all-purpose flour, whole wheat flour, cinnamon, ginger, baking soda, salt, and cloves. Stir into the butter mixture. Cover and chill in the refrigerator till firm enough to roll out.
	● Turn oven to 375°. Divide dough in half. Chill 1 half. On lightly floured surface roll out other half so it's ¼ inch thick. Cut with cookie cutters. Place 1 inch apart on ungreased cookie sheets. Repeat with remaining dough. Bake in the 375° oven 8 to 10 minutes or till edges are firm. Cool 1 minute. With pancake turner lift onto cooling rack.
1 8-ounce package cream cheese, softened 2 to 3 tablespoons honey Raisins, snipped dried apricots, *and* sunflower nuts	● For icing, mix softened cream cheese and honey till of piping consistency. Pipe icing onto cooled cookies. Decorate with raisins, apricots, and sunflower nuts. Store in refrigerator. Makes 24 cookies.

Rudolph's Antlers

1 6-ounce package (1 cup) semisweet chocolate pieces ½ of a 6-ounce package (½ cup) butterscotch pieces	● In a medium saucepan melt chocolate and butterscotch pieces over low heat, stirring occasionally. Remove from heat.
1 3-ounce can (2 cups) chow mein noodles	● Stir in chow mein noodles.
	● Drop by rounded teaspoons onto a waxed-paper-lined baking sheet, making V-shape cookies about 2 inches long.
12 maraschino cherries, halved	● Place a cherry half in the center of each. Chill in the refrigerator 1 to 2 hours or till firm. Makes 24 cookies.

Shape chocolate-covered chow mein noodles to look like reindeer antlers. There's no mistaking the red maraschino cherries for Rudolph's nose.

Sleds in the Snow

2 tablespoons butter *or* margarine	● Turn oven to 350°. Place the butter or margarine in a 9x9x2-inch baking pan. Place the pan in the oven to melt the butter. When the butter is melted, remove the pan.
1 cup packed brown sugar 1 cup chopped nuts ⅓ cup all-purpose flour ⅛ teaspoon baking soda ⅛ teaspoon salt	● In a medium mixing bowl stir together brown sugar, chopped nuts, flour, baking soda, and salt.
2 beaten eggs 1 teaspoon vanilla	● With a wooden spoon stir eggs and vanilla into nut mixture. Carefully pour the batter over the melted butter in the baking pan.
Sifted powdered sugar	● Bake in the 350° oven 20 to 25 minutes or till set. Sprinkle with powdered sugar. Place waxed paper under a cooling rack. Immediately turn pan upside down so bars come out onto the rack. Cool. Sprinkle again with powdered sugar. Cut into bars. Makes 24 bars.

Powdered sugar "snow" covers the bottoms and tops of these chewy bars.

Keep pot holders (and an adult helper) close by for taking the hot pan out of the oven and flipping the bars out of the pan.

Sweet treats hide inside these powdered sugar-coated cookies. Take a bite and see.

Surprise Snowballs

¾ cup butter *or* margarine (1½ sticks) ½ cup sugar ¼ teaspoon salt	● Turn oven to 350°. In a large mixer bowl beat butter or margarine with electric mixer on medium speed till softened (about 30 seconds). Add sugar and salt and beat till fluffy.
1 egg ½ teaspoon vanilla	● Add egg and vanilla. Beat well.
1¾ cups all-purpose flour	● With mixer on low speed gradually beat in flour till well mixed.
Candy-coated milk chocolate-covered peanuts, gumdrops, jelly beans, *and/or* candy-coated milk chocolate pieces	● Shape the dough into 1-inch balls. Press a piece of desired candy in center of each (see picture below) and shape the dough around it so you can't see the candy. Place balls about 2 inches apart on ungreased cookie sheets.
¾ cup sifted powdered sugar	● Bake in the 350° oven about 15 minutes or till edges are golden. Place powdered sugar in a plastic bag. With a pancake turner transfer 2 or 3 cookies at a time to the bag of powdered sugar. Gently shake cookies in powdered sugar till coated. Cool on a cooling rack. When cool, gently shake cookies again in powdered sugar. Makes about 36 cookies.

Shape these snowball cookies like real snowballs, only a lot smaller. Then hide a candy in each ball, bake, and shake in a plastic bag with powdered sugar till the cookies are coated. Shake them again after they've cooled.

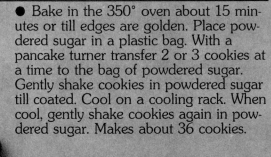

It's Spritz!

1½ cups butter *or* margarine (3 sticks) 1 cup sugar	● Turn oven to 400°. In a large mixer bowl beat butter or margarine with electric mixer on medium speed till softened (about 30 seconds). Add sugar and beat till fluffy.
1 egg 1 teaspoon vanilla ½ teaspoon almond extract (optional)	● Add egg, vanilla, and almond extract if desired. Beat well.
3½ cups all-purpose flour 1 teaspoon baking powder	● In a medium mixing bowl stir together flour and baking powder. With mixer on low speed gradually add flour mixture to butter mixture, beating till well mixed. Do not chill the dough.
Colored sugar, ground nuts, *or* decorative candies (optional)	● Force dough through cookie press onto ungreased cookie sheets. Decorate with colored sugar, ground nuts, or decorative candies if desired.
	● Bake in the 400° oven for 7 to 8 minutes or till edges are firm but not brown. With pancake turner lift cookies onto cooling rack. Makes about 60 cookies.

These butter cookies, commonly known as Spritz, are a holiday tradition in many homes. Like snowflakes, no two cookies are exactly alike. They're pretty just as they are or decorated with colored sugar, nuts, or decorative candies.

Before you fill the cookie press, pick the design plate you want to use and put it in place as the cookie press directions tell you. Then pack the dough in the tube.

Put the feet of the cookie press on the cookie sheet so the tube is straight up and down. Press out enough dough so it sticks to the cookie sheet but not so much that it squeezes out from under the press; lift off. Repeat for the other cookies. Sprinkle on any decorations *before* baking.

After the cookies are baked, use a pancake turner to lift them off the cookie sheets onto a cooling rack to cool. Store the cooled cookies in a plastic or metal container with a tight-fitting lid.

Giant Christmas-Card Cookies

1½ cups butter *or* margarine (3 sticks) 2 cups packed brown sugar	● In a large mixer bowl beat butter or margarine with electric mixer on medium speed till softened (about 30 seconds). Add brown sugar and beat till fluffy.
1 egg	● Add egg. Beat well.
4 cups all-purpose flour 2 teaspoons ground cinnamon 1 teaspoon ground nutmeg ½ teaspoon ground cloves ¼ teaspoon baking soda	● Stir together flour, cinnamon, nutmeg, cloves, and baking soda. With mixer on low speed gradually add flour mixture to butter mixture, beating well. Cover and chill in refrigerator about 2 hours or till firm enough to roll out.
Colored sugar *or* crushed sugar cubes (optional)	● Turn oven to 350°. For each cookie, roll ¾ *cup* of the chilled dough about ¼ inch thick directly onto an ungreased cookie sheet. (Keep remaining dough in the refrigerator.) Using floured cardboard patterns and a table knife, cut out desired shapes. Remove excess dough. Sprinkle cookies with colored sugar or crushed sugar cubes if desired.
	● Bake in the 350° oven for 10 to 12 minutes or till edges are browner than centers. Let cool on cookie sheets 8 minutes. With a pancake turner lift cookies onto a cooling rack to finish cooling.
Decorator icing Red cinnamon candies	● Decorate cookies with decorator icing and red cinnamon candies. Makes 8 to 10 large cookies.

Cookies so big you can fit only one or two on a cookie sheet. After you bake them, add a special icing message or decoration. Then give them away just like Christmas cards.

If you want to tie a ribbon in your cookie card, make a small hole in the top of the cookie before you bake it. After the cookie is baked and cooled, run a ribbon through the hole and tie a bow.

Roll the dough right onto the cookie sheet. Then, cut around cardboard patterns with a table knife. Reroll the dough scraps to use for another cookie.

Merry Christmas from Mary

Before making cookies, design 10x6-inch patterns (almost twice the size of cookies shown); cut out of cardboard. Rub a little flour on the patterns to keep them from sticking to the dough.

George Washington Cherry Cookies

¾ **cup butter *or* margarine (1½ sticks)** ¾ **cup sugar**	● Turn oven to 375°. In a large mixer bowl beat butter or margarine with electric mixer on medium speed till softened (about 30 seconds). Add sugar and beat till mixture is fluffy.
1 **egg** ¼ **cup cherry preserves**	● Add egg and the ¼ cup cherry preserves. Beat well.
2¼ **cups all-purpose flour** 1 **teaspoon baking soda** ½ **teaspoon salt**	● In a medium mixing bowl stir together the flour, baking soda, and salt. With electric mixer on low speed gradually add the flour mixture to the butter mixture, beating till well mixed.
	● Drop dough by rounded teaspoons about 2 inches apart onto ungreased cookie sheets.
	● Bake in the 375° oven for 8 to 10 minutes or till cookies are golden. Let cool on cookie sheets 1 minute. With a pancake turner lift cookies onto a cooling rack to finish cooling.
Cherry preserves	● When cool, top each cookie with a little additional cherry preserves. Makes about 48 cookies.

Celebrate George Washington's Birthday with cookies made with cherry preserves. Use preserves in the cookie dough and dab a little on top of the cookies after you've baked them.

We often use cherries to remember George Washington because as a boy he told his father the truth that he cut down the family's cherry tree. But more important than that are the things he did when he grew up to be the first president of the United States.

Shamrocks

¾ cup butter *or* margarine (1½ sticks) ⅔ cup sugar ¼ teaspoon salt	● In a large mixer bowl beat butter or margarine with electric mixer on medium speed till softened (about 30 seconds). Add sugar and salt and beat till fluffy.	**Fun cookies to make for St. Patrick's Day—or any day. Kids like the color o' green, sparkle o' green sugar, and flavor o' mint.**
1 egg ¼ teaspoon peppermint extract *or* vanilla Few drops green food coloring	● Add the egg, peppermint extract or vanilla, and a few drops of green food coloring. Beat mixture well.	
2 cups all-purpose flour	● With mixer on low speed gradually add flour to butter mixture and beat well.	
Green colored sugar	● Divide dough into 3 equal parts. Shape each part into a roll about 1 inch thick and about 8 inches long. Roll each in green colored sugar. Wrap rolls in clear plastic wrap. Chill in refrigerator at least 2 hours or up to 1 week.	**To shape each shamrock, place 3 slices of dough, sides touching, on an un-greased cookie sheet. Cut a stem from a fourth slice and attach to the sham-rock (save the rest of this slice for cutting other shamrock stems). With three fingers, gently push the slices together so each leaflet curves in slightly.**
	● Turn oven to 350°. Unwrap rolls. Slice crosswise so the slices are ¼ inch thick.	
	● Follow directions at right for shaping cookies.	
	● Bake in the 350° oven about 8 minutes or till edges are light brown. With a pancake turner lift the cookies onto a cooling rack to cool. Makes 32 cookies.	

The legend of the sham-rock says St. Patrick once used a 3-leaved shamrock to preach about the Holy Trinity and many who heard became Christians.

Easter Nests

½ cup butter *or* margarine (1 stick) 1 3-ounce package cream cheese ½ cup sugar ¼ teaspoon almond *or* lemon extract	● In a large mixer bowl beat butter or margarine and cream cheese with electric mixer on medium speed till softened (about 30 seconds). Add sugar and extract and beat till fluffy.	**Each buttery cookie is a coconut-covered nest that holds a jelly bean egg.**
1 cup all-purpose flour 2 teaspoons baking powder ¼ teaspoon salt	● In a medium mixing bowl stir together flour, baking powder, and salt. With mixer on low speed gradually add the flour mixture to the butter mixture, beating till well mixed.	
	● Cover and chill the dough in the refrigerator for 1 to 2 hours or till firm enough to handle.	
1 teaspoon water 4 or 5 drops green food coloring 1 3½-ounce can (1⅓ cups) flaked coconut	● Turn oven to 350°. In a screw-top jar combine water and food coloring. Add the coconut. Cover and shake till all the coconut is tinted.	**An easy way to tint the coconut is to put it in a jar with a little water and several drops of green food coloring. Screw on the lid and shake till all the coconut is green.**
	● Remove dough from refrigerator. With your hands, shape the dough into 1-inch balls. Roll each ball of dough in the tinted coconut till thoroughly coated. Place about 2 inches apart on ungreased cookie sheets.	
About 40 jelly beans	● Bake in the 350° oven for 12 to 15 minutes or till edges are firm. While cookies are still hot, press a jelly bean in the center of each cookie. With a pancake turner lift cookies onto a cooling rack to cool. Makes about 40 cookies.	

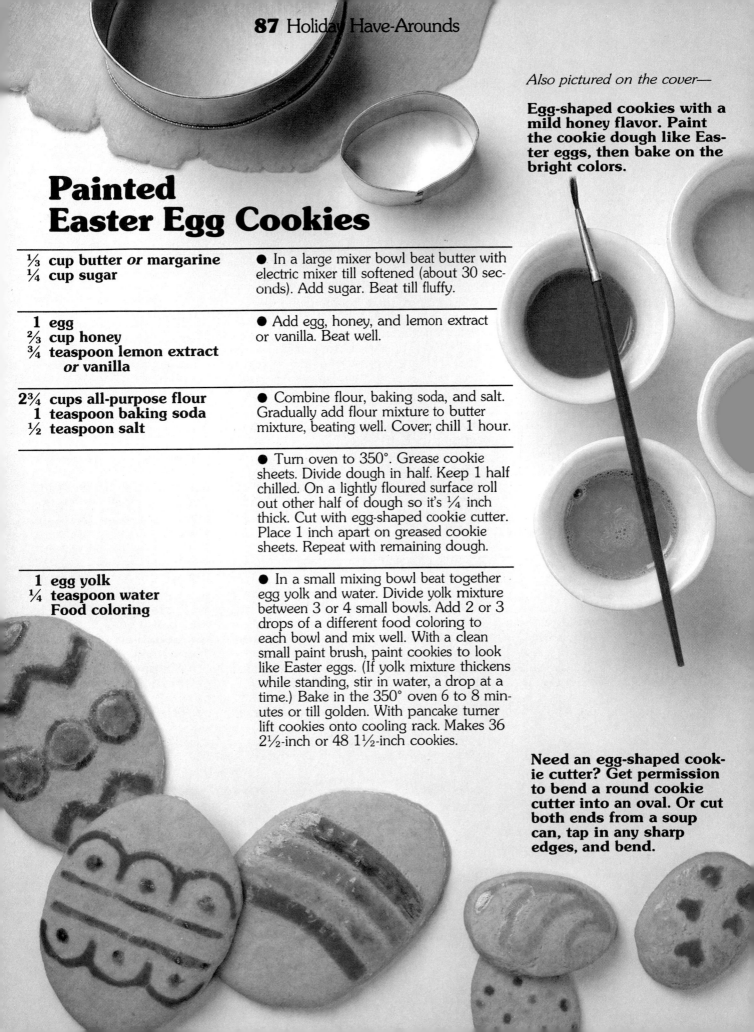

Also pictured on the cover—

Egg-shaped cookies with a mild honey flavor. Paint the cookie dough like Easter eggs, then bake on the bright colors.

Painted Easter Egg Cookies

⅓ cup butter *or* margarine ¼ cup sugar	● In a large mixer bowl beat butter with electric mixer till softened (about 30 seconds). Add sugar. Beat till fluffy.
1 egg ⅔ cup honey ¾ teaspoon lemon extract *or* vanilla	● Add egg, honey, and lemon extract or vanilla. Beat well.
2¾ cups all-purpose flour 1 teaspoon baking soda ½ teaspoon salt	● Combine flour, baking soda, and salt. Gradually add flour mixture to butter mixture, beating well. Cover; chill 1 hour.
	● Turn oven to 350°. Grease cookie sheets. Divide dough in half. Keep 1 half chilled. On a lightly floured surface roll out other half of dough so it's ¼ inch thick. Cut with egg-shaped cookie cutter. Place 1 inch apart on greased cookie sheets. Repeat with remaining dough.
1 egg yolk ¼ teaspoon water Food coloring	● In a small mixing bowl beat together egg yolk and water. Divide yolk mixture between 3 or 4 small bowls. Add 2 or 3 drops of a different food coloring to each bowl and mix well. With a clean small paint brush, paint cookies to look like Easter eggs. (If yolk mixture thickens while standing, stir in water, a drop at a time.) Bake in the 350° oven 6 to 8 minutes or till golden. With pancake turner lift cookies onto cooling rack. Makes 36 2½-inch or 48 1½-inch cookies.

Need an egg-shaped cookie cutter? Get permission to bend a round cookie cutter into an oval. Or cut both ends from a soup can, tap in any sharp edges, and bend.

4th of July Flags

½ **cup butter *or* margarine (1 stick)** ½ **cup shortening** ½ **cup sugar** ½ **cup packed brown sugar**	● In a large mixer bowl beat butter or margarine and shortening with electric mixer on medium speed about 30 seconds. Add sugar and brown sugar and beat till fluffy.
1 egg **2 tablespoons milk** ½ **teaspoon vanilla**	● Add egg, milk, and vanilla. Beat well.
2¼ **cups all-purpose flour** ½ **teaspoon baking soda** ½ **teaspoon salt**	● In a medium mixing bowl stir together flour, baking soda, and salt. With mixer on low speed gradually add flour mixture to butter mixture, beating till well mixed.
⅛ **to** ¼ **teaspoon red paste food coloring**	● Divide dough in half. To *one* half, add food coloring and stir till well mixed. Follow directions at right for layering dough.
Canned creamy white frosting **Blue colored sugar *or* blue decorator icing**	● Turn oven to 375°. Follow directions below for slicing dough. Place slices 1 inch apart on ungreased cookie sheets. Bake in the 375° oven 8 to 10 minutes or till edges are golden. With pancake turner lift cookies onto cooling rack to cool. In upper left corner of each flag, spread a 1-inch square of white frosting. Decorate with colored sugar or decorator icing. Makes about 36.

Fly these flags at a 4th of July celebration. Star-spangle the banners with decorator icing or colored sugar sprinkled through a tiny cookie cutter.

Put a piece of waxed paper in the bottom and up 2 sides of an 8x4x2-inch loaf pan. Press *half* of the red dough evenly in pan. Top with *half* of the plain dough, patting evenly. Repeat red and plain layers, patting each evenly. Cover. Freeze at least 4 hours.

Grasp the waxed paper to lift the dough out of the loaf pan. With a sharp knife, slice the dough crosswise into 3 equal parts. Then, starting at the short end of each part, cut crosswise into ¼-inch-thick slices.

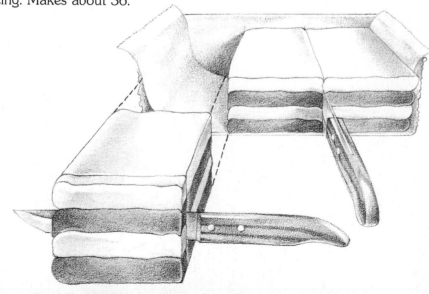

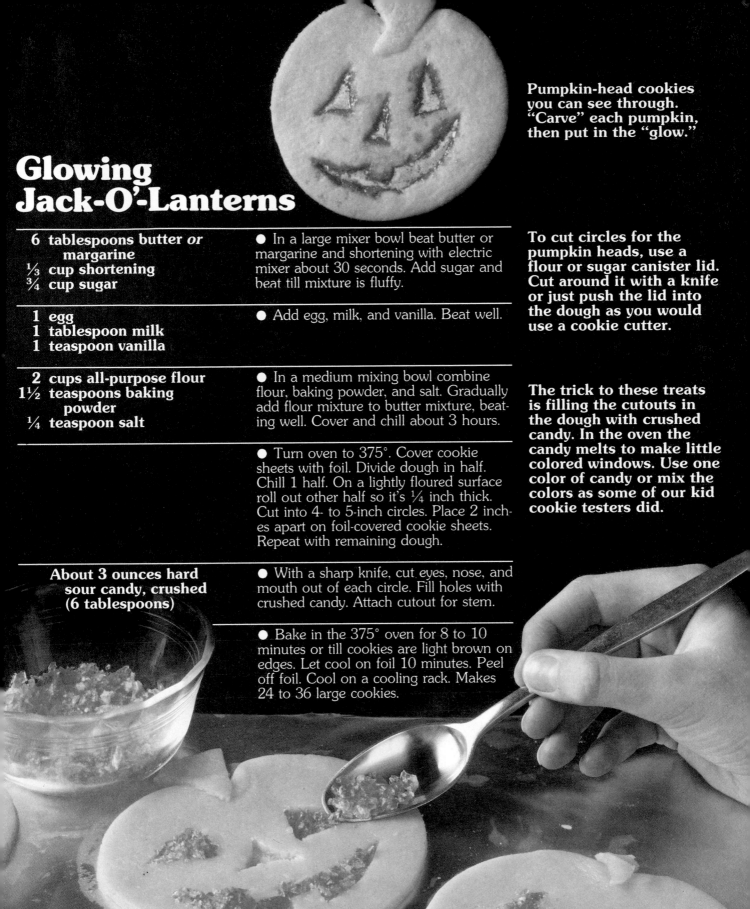

Glowing Jack-O'-Lanterns

Pumpkin-head cookies you can see through. "Carve" each pumpkin, then put in the "glow."

6 **tablespoons butter** *or* **margarine** ⅓ **cup shortening** ¾ **cup sugar**	● In a large mixer bowl beat butter or margarine and shortening with electric mixer about 30 seconds. Add sugar and beat till mixture is fluffy.
1 **egg** 1 **tablespoon milk** 1 **teaspoon vanilla**	● Add egg, milk, and vanilla. Beat well.
2 **cups all-purpose flour** 1½ **teaspoons baking powder** ¼ **teaspoon salt**	● In a medium mixing bowl combine flour, baking powder, and salt. Gradually add flour mixture to butter mixture, beating well. Cover and chill about 3 hours.
	● Turn oven to 375°. Cover cookie sheets with foil. Divide dough in half. Chill 1 half. On a lightly floured surface roll out other half so it's ¼ inch thick. Cut into 4- to 5-inch circles. Place 2 inches apart on foil-covered cookie sheets. Repeat with remaining dough.
About 3 ounces hard sour candy, crushed (6 tablespoons)	● With a sharp knife, cut eyes, nose, and mouth out of each circle. Fill holes with crushed candy. Attach cutout for stem.
	● Bake in the 375° oven for 8 to 10 minutes or till cookies are light brown on edges. Let cool on foil 10 minutes. Peel off foil. Cool on a cooling rack. Makes 24 to 36 large cookies.

To cut circles for the pumpkin heads, use a flour or sugar canister lid. Cut around it with a knife or just push the lid into the dough as you would use a cookie cutter.

The trick to these treats is filling the cutouts in the dough with crushed candy. In the oven the candy melts to make little colored windows. Use one color of candy or mix the colors as some of our kid cookie testers did.

Oriental treats made in a frying pan. First, youngsters can enjoy writing fortunes. Then, adults can have the honorable job of frying the cookies.

Good Fortune Cookies

¼ cup all-purpose flour 2 tablespoons sugar 1 tablespoon cornstarch Dash salt	● Before making the cookies, write fortunes on strips of paper ½ inch wide and about 6 inches long. In a small mixing bowl stir together flour, sugar, cornstarch, and salt.
2 tablespoons cooking oil 1 egg white	● Add cooking oil and egg white and stir till mixture is smooth.
1 tablespoon water ½ teaspoon vanilla	● Add water and vanilla. Stir well.
	● Lightly grease a skillet or griddle with cooking oil. Make 1 cookie at a time. For each cookie, pour *1 tablespoon* of the batter in the skillet or griddle and spread to a 4-inch circle. Cook over medium-low heat about 4 minutes or till light brown. Turn with wide pancake turner and cook 15 seconds more. Working quickly, follow directions below for shaping cookies. Makes 8 cookies.

Before you make the cookies, write fortunes, wise sayings, or wisecracks on strips of paper. Then make the cookies, tucking in the fortune before you fold them up.

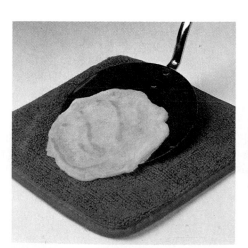

When the cookie is done on both sides, use a wide pancake turner to lift it out of the skillet onto a pot holder.

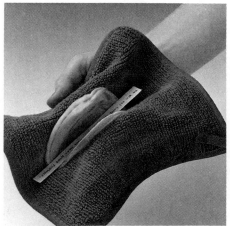

Working quickly while the cookie is still soft, put a fortune in the middle and fold the cookie in half.

Bend the folded side in half over the edge of a bowl. Gently pull on the ends so edges of cookie come together. Put in a muffin pan to cool.

Mexican Wedding Cakes

1 cup butter *or* margarine (2 sticks)	● Turn oven to 325°. In a large mixer bowl beat butter or margarine with electric mixer on medium speed till softened (about 30 seconds).	These buttery balls have a double coating of powdered sugar. If you can, let them melt in your mouth. But you'll find this hard to do because they taste so good!
½ cup sifted powdered sugar 1 teaspoon vanilla	● Add the ½ cup powdered sugar and the vanilla and beat till fluffy.	
2 cups all-purpose flour ½ cup finely chopped pecans ⅛ teaspoon salt	● In a medium mixing bowl stir together flour, finely chopped pecans, and salt. With mixer on low speed gradually add flour mixture to butter mixture, beating till well mixed.	The Mexican people like desserts, probably because their mouths need a rest from the spicy food they often eat. *Mexican Wedding Cakes* are called *polvorones* by Mexicans and are one way of ending a meal in a sweet way.
	● With your hands, shape dough into 1-inch balls. Place balls about 1 inch apart on ungreased cookie sheets.	
About 1 cup sifted powdered sugar	● Bake in the 325° oven about 20 minutes or till light brown. Place the powdered sugar in a plastic bag. With a pancake turner transfer 2 or 3 cookies at a time to the powdered sugar in the bag. Shake cookies in powdered sugar till coated. Cool on a cooling rack.	Russians have their own version of these popular cookies, and they call them Russian Tea Cakes. Their cookies have the same buttery goodness but often they are formed into finger shapes as well as balls.
	● When cookies have cooled, shake again in the powdered sugar. Makes about 42 cookies.	

Dutch Spice Cookies

1 cup butter *or* margarine (2 sticks)
1½ cups packed brown sugar

● In a large mixer bowl beat butter or margarine with electric mixer on medium speed till softened (about 30 seconds). Add brown sugar and beat till fluffy.

1 egg

● Add egg. Beat well.

3½ cups all-purpose flour
2 teaspoons ground cinnamon
1 teaspoon ground nutmeg
½ teaspoon ground cloves

● In a medium mixing bowl stir together flour, cinnamon, nutmeg, and cloves. With mixer on low speed gradually add flour mixture to butter mixture, beating till well mixed. Cover and chill in the refrigerator about 1 hour or till firm enough to handle.

● Turn oven to 350°. Roll the dough into 1-inch balls. Place balls about 2 inches apart on ungreased cookie sheets. Flatten with floured cookie stamp or the bottom of a drinking glass that has a design in it.

● Bake in the 350° oven for 8 to 10 minutes or till light brown on bottom. With pancake turner lift cookies onto a cooling rack to cool. Store in a tightly covered container. Makes about 36.

In Holland, spice cookies are shaped in molds to make windmills or other figures. Make patterns in your cookies with a cookie stamp or a glass with a grooved bottom.

We had as much fun watching 3 kids make *Dutch Spice Cookies* as they had making them. One of them, who liked squeezing the dough through her fingers, said, "It smells like nutmeg." A tiny 6-year-old pinched off a piece of dough, popped it in her mouth, and remarked, "That's good dough." When the kids lifted the stamp from the dough and found the designs they'd made, one of them burst out, "Look at that—neat!"

English Tea Biscuits

Pictured on page 8—

½ cup butter *or* margarine (1 stick) ½ cup sugar 1 teaspoon finely shredded lemon peel	● Turn oven to 375°. In a large mixer bowl beat butter or margarine with electric mixer on medium speed till softened (about 30 seconds). Add sugar and lemon peel and beat till fluffy.
1 egg 2 tablespoons lemon juice	● Add egg and lemon juice. Beat well.
1¼ cups all-purpose flour ½ teaspoon baking powder ¼ teaspoon salt	● In a medium mixing bowl stir together flour, baking powder, and salt. With electric mixer on low speed gradually add the flour mixture to the butter mixture, beating till well mixed.
½ cup currants	● With a wooden spoon stir in currants.
	● Drop the dough by rounded teaspoons about 2 inches apart onto ungreased cookie sheets.
	● Bake in the 375° oven for 8 to 10 minutes or till edges of cookies are light brown. With a pancake turner lift cookies onto a cooling rack to cool. Makes about 30 cookies.

People in England call cookies "biscuits." These lemony drop cookies have currants in them, a fruit that will remind you of tart little raisins. If you like, you can use the same amount of raisins instead of the currants.

Every day the English people take a late-afternoon break called "tea." They serve tea and something to eat to tide them over till dinner, a lot like our afternoon snacks in America. They might serve rolls with jam, little sandwiches, or something on the sweet side, such as these tea biscuits.

Index